ARCHITECT REGISTRATION EXAM

SCHEMATIC DESIGN

ARE SAMPLE PROBLEMS AND PRACTICE EXAM

DAVID KENT BALLAST, FAIA

The Power to Pass™
www.ppl2pass.com

Professional Publications, Inc. • Belmont, California

Benefit by Registering This Book with PPI

- Get book updates and corrections
- Hear the latest exam news
- Obtain exclusive exam tips and strategies
- Receive special discounts

Register your book at **www.ppi2pass.com/register**.

Report Errors and View Corrections for This Book

PPI is grateful to every reader who notifies us of a possible error. Your feedback allows us to improve the quality and accuracy of our products. You can report errata and view corrections at **www.ppi2pass.com/errata**.

SCHEMATIC DESIGN:
ARE SAMPLE PROBLEMS AND PRACTICE EXAM

Current printing of this edition: 3

Printing History

edition number	printing number	update
1	1	New book.
1	2	Minor corrections.
1	3	Minor corrections.

Printed in the United States of America

PPI
1250 Fifth Avenue, Belmont, CA 94002
(650) 593-9119
www.ppi2pass.com

ISBN: 978-1-59126-125-4

TABLE OF CONTENTS

PREFACE AND ACKNOWLEDGMENTS

This book is tailored to the needs of those studying for version 4.0 of the Architect Registration Examination. The ARE 4.0 is one step in a process of change that began in 2001, when the National Council of Architectural Registration Boards (NCARB) published the results of a two-year study of the architecture profession. Since then, in response to that study, NCARB has introduced a series of changes to the ARE. Previous versions of the ARE have reduced the number of graphic vignettes and introduced new types of questions. Version 4.0, though, is the most substantial change yet, reorganizing and reducing the number of divisions and integrating graphic vignettes into divisions that were previously multiple choice only.

In the ARE 4.0, NCARB has eliminated the graphics-only Building Technology division and redistributed its six graphic vignettes into other divisions, combining them with multiple-choice sections of the exam. Each multiple-choice section carried over from version 3.1 now contains fewer questions, and a multiple-choice section has been added to the Site Planning & Design division (formerly called just Site Planning). The two structural divisions from version 3.1, General Structures and Lateral Forces, are now combined into one division, Structural Systems. In all, there are now seven divisions instead of nine, and there are somewhat fewer multiple-choice questions in all on the ARE 4.0 than on version 3.1.

In response to the version 4.0 changes, PPI has reorganized and revised its ARE review books. *ARE Review Manual* now covers all the divisions of the ARE in a single volume. This new book, *Schematic Design: ARE Sample Problems and Practice Exam*, is one of seven companion volumes, one for each ARE 4.0 division. We believe that this organization will help you study for individual divisions most effectively.

You will find that this book and the related volumes are valuable parts of your exam preparation. Although there is no substitute for a good formal education and the broad-based experience provided by your internship with a practicing architect, this review series will help direct your study efforts to increase your chances of passing the ARE.

Many people have helped in the production of this book. I would like to thank all the fine people at PPI including Scott Marley (project editor), Amy Schwertman (typesetter, cover designer, and illustrator), and Thomas Bergstrom (illustrator).

David Kent Ballast, FAIA

INTRODUCTION

ABOUT THIS BOOK

Schematic Design: ARE Sample Problems and Practice Exam is written to help you prepare for the Schematic Design division of the Architect Registration Examination (ARE), version 4.0.

Although this book can be a valuable study aid by itself, it is designed to be used along with the *ARE Review Manual*, also published by PPI. The *ARE Review Manual* is organized into sections that cover all seven divisions of the ARE 4.0.

- Programming, Planning & Practice
- Site Planning & Design
- Schematic Design
- Structural Systems
- Building Systems
- Building Design & Construction Systems
- Construction Documents & Services

This book is one of seven companion volumes to the *ARE Review Manual* that PPI publishes. Each of these books contains sample problems and practice exams for one of the ARE 4.0 divisions.

- *Programming, Planning & Practice: ARE Sample Problems and Practice Exam*
- *Site Planning & Design: ARE Sample Problems and Practice Exam*
- *Schematic Design: ARE Sample Problems and Practice Exam*
- *Structural Systems: ARE Sample Problems and Practice Exam*
- *Building Systems: ARE Sample Problems and Practice Exam*
- *Building Design & Construction Systems: ARE Sample Problems and Practice Exam*
- *Construction Documents & Services: ARE Sample Problems and Practice Exam*

THE ARCHITECT REGISTRATION EXAMINATION

Congratulations on completing (or nearing the end of) the Intern Development Program! You are two-thirds of the way to being able to call yourself an architect. NAAB degree? Check. IDP? Check. Now on to step three.

The final hurdle is the Architect Registration Examination. The ARE is a uniform test administered to candidates who wish to become licensed architects after they have served their required internships. It is given in all fifty states, all ten Canadian provinces, and five other jurisdictions including the District of Columbia, Guam, the Northern Mariana Islands, Puerto Rico, and the Virgin Islands.

The ARE has been developed to protect the health, safety, and welfare of the public by testing a candidate's entry-level competence to practice architecture. Its content relates as closely as possible to situations encountered in practice. It tests for the kinds of knowledge, skills, and abilities required of an entry-level architect, with particular emphasis on those services that affect public health, safety, and welfare. In order to accomplish these objectives, the exam tests for

- knowledge in specific subject areas
- the ability to make decisions
- the ability to consolidate and use information to solve a problem
- the ability to coordinate the activities of others on the building team

The ARE also includes some professional practice and project management questions.

The ARE is developed jointly by the National Council of Architectural Registration Boards (NCARB) and the Committee of Canadian Architectural Councils (CCAC), with the assistance of the Chauncey Group International and Prometric. The Chauncey Group serves as NCARB's test development and operations consultant, and Prometric operates and maintains the test centers where the ARE is administered.

Although the responsibility of professional licensing rests with each individual state, every state's board requires successful completion of the ARE to achieve registration or licensure. One of the primary reasons for a uniform test is to facilitate reciprocity—that is, to enable an architect to more easily gain a license to practice in states other than the one in which he or she was originally licensed.

The ARE is administered and graded entirely by computer. All divisions of the exam are offered six days a week at a network of test centers across North America. The results are scored by computer, and the results are forwarded to individual state boards of architecture, which process them and send them to candidates. If you fail a division, you must wait six months before you can retake that division.

First Steps

As you begin to prepare for the exam, you should first obtain a current copy of *ARE Guidelines* from NCARB. This booklet will get you started with the exam process and will be a valuable reference throughout. It includes descriptions of the seven divisions, instructions on how to apply, pay for, and take the ARE, and other useful information. You can download a PDF version at www.ncarb.org, or you can request a printed copy through the contact information provided at that site.

The NCARB website also gives current information about the exam, education requirements, training, examination procedures, and NCARB reciprocity services. It includes sample scenarios of the computer-based examination process and examples of costs associated with taking the computer-based exam.

The PPI website is also a good source of exam info (at **www.ppi2pass.com/areinfo**) and answers to frequently asked questions (at **www.ppi2pass.com/arefaq**).

To register as an examinee, you should obtain the registration requirements from the board in the state, province, or territory where you want to be registered. The exact requirements vary from one jurisdiction to another, so contact your local board. Links to state boards can be found at **www.ppi2pass.com/areinfo**.

As soon as NCARB has verified your qualifications and you have received your "Authorization to Test" letter, you may begin scheduling examinations. The exams are offered on a first come, first served basis and must be scheduled at least 72 hours in advance. See *ARE Guidelines* for instructions on finding a current list of testing centers. You may take the exams at any location, even outside the state in which you intend to become registered.

You may schedule any division of the ARE at any time and may take the divisions in any order. Divisions can be taken one at a time, to spread out preparation time and exam costs, or can be taken together in any combination.

However, each candidate must pass all seven divisions of the ARE within a single five-year period. This period, or "rolling clock," begins on the date of the first division you passed. If you have not completed the ARE within five years, the divisions that you passed more than five years ago are no longer credited, and the content in them must be retaken. Your new five-year period begins on the date of the earliest division you passed within the last five years.

About the ARE 4.0

NCARB's introduction of ARE version 4.0 in July 2008 marked the change to an exam format with both multiple-choice and graphic subjects appearing within the same division. In the previous version, the ARE 3.1, each division contained either multiple-choice problems or graphic problems, never both.

The ARE 4.0 also has fewer divisions than the ARE 3.1, seven instead of nine. The organization of the ARE 4.0 exam means that candidates will make fewer trips to the test center, and can study for related portions of the exam all at once.

Examination Format

The ARE 4.0 is organized into seven divisions that test various areas of architectural knowledge and problem-solving ability.

Programming, Planning & Practice

85 multiple-choice questions
1 graphic vignette: Site Zoning

Site Planning & Design

65 multiple-choice questions
2 graphic vignettes: Site Design, Site Grading

Schematic Design

2 graphic vignettes: Building Layout, Interior Layout

Structural Systems

125 multiple-choice questions
1 graphic vignette: Structural Layout

Building Systems

95 multiple-choice questions
1 graphic vignette: Mechanical & Electrical Plan

Building Design & Construction Systems

85 multiple-choice questions
3 graphic vignettes: Accessibility/Ramp, Roof Plan, Stair Design

Construction Documents & Services

100 multiple-choice questions
1 graphic vignette: Building Section

Experienced test-takers will tell you that there is quite a bit of overlap among these divisions. Questions that seem better suited to the Construction Documents & Services division may show up on the Building Design & Construction Systems division, for example, and questions on architectural history and building regulations might show up anywhere. That's why it's important to have a comprehensive strategy for studying and taking the exams.

The ARE is given entirely by computer. There are two kinds of problems on the exam. Multiple-choice problems are short questions presented on the computer screen; you answer them by clicking on the right answer or answers, or by filling in a blank. Graphic vignettes are longer problems in design; you solve a vignette by planning and drawing your solution on the computer. Six of the seven divisions contain both multiple-choice sections and graphic vignettes; the Schematic Design division contains only vignettes. Both kinds of problems are described later in this Introduction.

STUDY GUIDELINES

After the five to seven years (or even more) of higher education you've received to this point, you probably have a good idea of the study strategy that works best for you. The trick is figuring out how to apply that to the ARE. Unlike many college courses, there isn't a textbook or set of class notes from which all the exam questions will be derived. The exams are very broad and draw questions from multiple areas of knowledge.

The first challenge, then, is figuring out what to study. The ARE is never quite the same exam twice. The field of knowledge tested is always the same, but the specific questions asked are drawn randomly from a large pool, and will differ from one candidate to the next. One division may contains many code-related questions for one candidate and only a few for the next. This makes the ARE a challenge to study for.

ARE Guidelines contains lists of resources recommended by NCARB. That list can seem overwhelming, though, and on top of that, many of the recommended books are expensive or no longer in print. To help address this problem, a number of publishers sell study guides for the ARE. These guides summarize the information found in primary sources such as the NCARB-recommended books. A list of helpful resources for preparing for the Schematic Design division can also be found in the Recommended Reading section of this book.

Your method of studying for the ARE should be based on both the content and form of the exam and on your school and work experience. Because the exam covers such a broad range of subject matter, it cannot possibly include every detail of practice. Rather, it tends to focus on what is considered entry-level knowledge and knowledge that is important for the protection of the public's health, safety, and welfare. Other types of questions are asked, too, but this knowledge should be the focus of your review schedule.

Your recent work experience should also help you determine what areas to study the most. A candidate who has been involved with construction documents for several years will probably need less review in that area than in others he or she has not had recent experience with.

The *ARE Review Manual* and its companion volumes are structured to help candidates focus on the topics that are more likely to be included in the exam in one form or another. Some subjects may seem familiar or may be easy to recall from memory, and others may seem completely foreign; the latter are the ones to give particular attention to. It may be wise to study additional sources on these subjects, take review seminars, or get special help from someone who is knowledgeable in the topic.

A typical candidate might spend about forty hours preparing for and taking each exam. Some will need to study more, some less. Forty hours is about one week of studying eight hours a day, or two weeks of four hours a day, or a month of two hours a day, along with reasonable breaks and time to attend to other responsibilities. As you probably work full time and have other family and personal obligations, it is important to develop a realistic schedule and do your best to stick to it. The ARE is not the kind of exam you can cram for the night before.

Also, since the fees are high and retaking a test is expensive, you want to do your best and pass in as few tries as possible. Allowing enough time to study and going into each exam well prepared will help you relax and concentrate on the questions.

The following steps may provide a useful structure for an exam study program.

Step 1: Start early. You can't review for a test like this by starting two weeks before the date. This is especially true if you are taking all portions of the exam for the first time.

Step 2: Go through the *ARE Review Manual* quickly to get a feeling for the scope of the subject matter and how the major topics are organized. Whatever division you're studying for, plan to review the chapters on building regulations as well. Review *ARE Guidelines*.

Step 3: Based on your review of the *ARE Review Manual* and *ARE Guidelines*, and on a realistic appraisal of your strong and weak areas, set priorities for study and determine which topics need more study time.

Step 4: Divide review subjects into manageable units and organize them into a sequence of study. It is generally best to start with the less familiar subjects. Based on the exam date and plans for beginning study, assign a time limit to each study unit. Again, your knowledge of a subject should determine the time devoted to it. You may want to devote an entire week to earthquake design if it is an unfamiliar subject, and only one day to timber design if it is a familiar one. In setting up a schedule, be realistic about other life commitments as well as your personal ability to concentrate on studying over a length of time.

Step 5: Begin studying, and stick with the schedule. Of course, this is the most difficult part of the process and the one that requires the most self-discipline. The job should be easier if you have started early and if you are following a realistic schedule that allows time for recreation and personal commitments.

Step 6: Stop studying a day or two before the exam. Relax. By this time, no amount of additional cramming will help.

At some point in your studying, you will want to spend some time becoming familiar with the program you will be using to solve the graphic vignettes, which does not resemble commercial CAD software. The software and sample vignettes can be downloaded from the NCARB website at www.ncarb.org.

There are many schools of thought on the best order for taking the divisions. One factor to consider is the six-month waiting period before you can retake a particular division. It's never fun to predict what you might fail, but if you know that a specific area might give you trouble, consider taking that exam near the beginning. You might be pleasantly surprised when you check the mailbox, but if not, as you work through the rest of the exams, the clock will be ticking and you can schedule the retest six months later.

Here are some additional tips.

- Learn concepts first, and then details later. For example, it is much better to understand the basic ideas and theories of waterproofing than it is to attempt to memorize dozens of waterproofing products and details. Once the concept is clear, the details are much easier to learn and to apply during the exam.

- Use the index to the *ARE Review Manual* to focus on particular subjects in which you feel weak, especially subjects that can apply to more than one division.

- Don't tackle all your hardest subjects first. Make one of your early exams one that you feel fairly confident about. It's nice to get off on the right foot with a PASS.

- Programming, Planning & Practice and Building Design & Construction Systems both tend to be "catch-all" divisions that cover a lot of material from the Construction Documents & Services division as well as others. Consider taking Construction Documents & Services first among those three, and then the other two soon after.

- Many past candidates recommend taking the Programming, Planning & Practice division last or nearly last, so that you will be familiar with the body of knowledge for all the other divisions as well.

- Brush up on architectural history before taking any of the divisions with multiple-choice sections. Know major buildings and their architects, particularly structures that are representative of an architect's philosophy (for example, Le Corbusier and the Villa Savoye) or that represent "firsts" or "turning points."

- Try to schedule your exams so that you'll have enough time to get yourself ready, eat, and review a little. If you'll have a long drive to the testing center, try to avoid having to make it during rush hour.

- If you are planning to take more than one division at a time, do not overstudy any one portion of the exam. It is generally better to review the concepts than to try to become an overnight expert in one area. For example, the exam may ask general questions about plate girders, but it will not ask for a complete, detailed design of a plate girder.

- Solve as many sample problems as possible, including those provided with NCARB's practice program, the books of sample problems and practice exams published by PPI, and any others that are available.

- Take advantage of the community of intern architects going through this experience with you. Some local AIA chapters offer ARE preparation courses or may be able to help you organize a study group with other interns in your area. Visit website forums to discuss the exam with others who have taken it or are preparing to take it. The Architecture Exam Forum at **www.ppi2pass.com/areforum** is a great online resource for questions, study advice, and encouragement. Even though the ARE questions change daily, it is a good idea to get a feeling for the types of questions that are being asked, the general emphasis, and the subject areas that previous candidates have found particularly troublesome.

- A day or two before the first test session, stop studying in order to relax as much as possible. Get plenty of sleep the night before the test.

- Try to relax as much as possible during study periods and during the exam itself. Worrying is counterproductive. Candidates who have worked diligently in school, have obtained a wide range of experience during internship, and have started exam review early will be in the best possible position to pass the ARE.

TAKING THE EXAM

What to Bring

Bring multiple forms of photo ID and your Authorization to Test letter to the test site.

It is neither necessary nor permitted to bring any reference materials or scratch paper into the test site. Pencils and scratch paper are provided by the proctor and must be returned when leaving the exam room. Earplugs will also be provided. Leave all your books and notes in the car. Most testing centers have lockers for your keys, small personal belongings, and cell phone.

Do not bring a calculator into the test site. A calculator built into the testing software will be available in all divisions.

Arriving at the Testing Center

Allow plenty of time to get to the exam site, to avoid transportation problems such as getting lost or stuck in traffic jams. If you can, arrive a little early, and take a little time in the parking lot to review one last time the formulas and other things you need to memorize. Then relax, take a few deep breaths, and go take the exam.

Once at the testing center, you will check in with the attendant, who will verify your identification and your Authorization to Test. (Don't forget to take this home with you after each exam; you'll need it for the next one.) After you check in, you'll be shown to your testing station.

When the exam begins, you will have the opportunity to click through a tutorial that explains how the computer program works. You'll probably want to read through it the first time, but after that initial exam, you will know how the software works and you won't need the tutorial. Take a deep breath, organize your paper and pencils, and take advantage of the opportunity to dump all the facts floating around in your brain onto your scratch paper—write down as much as you can. This includes formulas, ratios ("if x increases, y decreases"), and so on—anything that you are trying desperately not to forget. If you can get all the things you've crammed at the last minute onto that paper, you'll be able to think a little more clearly about the problems posed on the screen.

Solving the Vignettes

Each of the eleven graphic vignettes on the ARE is designed to test a particular area of knowledge and skill. Each one presents a base plan of some kind and gives programmatic and other requirements. The candidate must create a plan that satisfies the requirements.

The Building Layout vignette presents a site plan, a program, and code requirements, and requires the candidate to produce floor plans for a small, two-story building on the site. The candidate must satisfy the requirements while considering relevant features and limitations of the site.

The Interior Layout vignette tests the candidate's understanding of the principles of design and accessibility that govern basic interior space planning. A background floor plan is present, along with a program and code requirements. The candidate must plan the required spaces, including furniture, and show access to these spaces.

The computer scores the vignettes by a complex grading method. Design criteria are given various point values, and responses are categorized as Acceptable, Unacceptable, or Indeterminate.

General Tips for the Vignettes

Here are some general tips for approaching the vignettes. More detailed solving tips can be found in the solutions to each vignette.

- Remember that with the current format and computer grading, each vignette covers only a very specific area of knowledge and offers a limited number of possible solutions. In a few cases only one solution is really possible. Use this as an advantage.

- Read the problem thoroughly, twice. Follow the requirements exactly, letting each problem solve itself as much as possible. Be careful not to read more into the problem than is there. The test writers are very specific about what they want; there is no need to add to the problem requirements. If a particular type of solution is strongly suggested, follow that lead.

- Consider only those code requirements given in the vignette, even if they deviate from familiar codes. Do not read anything more into the problem. The code requirements may be slightly different from what candidates use in practice.

- Use the scratch paper provided to sketch possible solutions before starting the final solution.

- Make sure all programmed elements are included in the final design.

- When the functional requirements of the problem have been solved, use the problem statement as a checklist to make sure all criteria have been satisfied.

General Tips for Using the Vignette Software

It is important to practice with the vignette software that will be used in the exam. The program is unique to the ARE and unlike standard CAD software. If you are unfamiliar with the software interface you will waste valuable time learning to use it, and are likely to run out of time before completing the vignettes. Practice software can be downloaded at no charge from NCARB's website at www.ncarb.org. Usage time for the practice program can also be purchased at Prometric test centers. The practice software includes tutorials, directions, and one practice vignette for each of the eleven vignettes.

Here are some general tips for using the vignette software.

- When elements overlap on the screen, it may be difficult to select a particular element. If this happens, repeatedly click on the element without moving the mouse until the desire element is highlighted.

- Try to stay in "ortho" mode. This mode can be used to solve most problems, and it makes the solution process much easier and quicker. Unless obviously required by the vignette, creating additional angles complicates any problem with the time restrictions given.

- If the vignette relates to contour modifications, it may help to draw schematic sections through the significant existing slopes. This provides a three-dimensional image of the problem.

- When drawing, if the program states that elements should connect, make sure they touch at their boundaries only and do not overlap. Use the *check* tool to determine if there are any overlaps. Walls that do not align correctly can cause a solution to be downgraded or even rejected. Remember, walls between spaces change color temporarily when properly aligned.

- Make liberal use of the *zoom* tool for sizing and aligning components accurately. Zoom in as closely as possible on the area being worked. When aligning objects, it is also helpful to use the full-screen cursor.

- Turn on the grid and verify spacing. This makes it easier to align objects and get a sense of the sizes of objects and the distances between them. Use the *measure* tool to check exact measurements if needed.

- Make liberal use of the sketch tools. These can be turned on and off and do not count during the grading, but they can be used to show relationships and for temporary guidelines and other notations.

- Use sketch circles to show required distances, setbacks, clearances, and similar measures.

AFTER THE EXAM

When you've clicked the button to end the test, the computer may prompt you to provide some demographic information about yourself and your education and experience. Then gather your belongings, turn in your scratch paper and materials—you must leave them with the proctor—and leave the testing center. (For security reasons, you can't remove anything from the test center.) If the staff has retained your Authorization to Test and your identification, don't forget to retrieve both.

If you should encounter any problems during the exams or have any concerns, be sure to report them to the test center administrator and to NCARB as soon as possible. If you wait longer than ten days after you test, NCARB will not respond to your complaint. You must report your complaint immediately and directly to NCARB and copy your state registration board for any hope of assistance.

Then it's all over but the wait for the mail. How long it takes to get your scores will vary with the efficiency of your state registration board, which reviews the scores from NCARB before passing along the results. But four to six weeks is typical.

As you may have heard from classmates and colleagues, the ARE is a difficult exam—but it is certainly not impossible to pass. A solid architectural education and a well-rounded internship are the best preparation you can have. Watch carefully and listen to the vocabulary used by architects with more experience. Look for opportunities to participate in all phases of project delivery so that you have some "real world" experience to apply to the scenarios you will inevitably find in exam questions.

One last piece of advice is not to put off taking the exams. Take them as soon as you become eligible. You will probably still remember a little bit from your college courses and you may even have your old textbooks and notes handy. As life gets more complicated—with spouses and children and work obligations—it is easy to make excuses and never find time to get around to it. Make the commitment, and do it now. After all, this is the last step to reaching your goal of calling yourself an architect.

HOW TO USE THIS BOOK

This book contains four sample vignettes and one complete practice exam consisting of two vignettes. These have been written to help you prepare for the Schematic Design division of the Architect Registration Examination, version 4.0.

One of the best ways to prepare for the ARE is by solving sample problems. While you are studying for this division, use the sample vignettes in this book to make yourself familiar with the kind of problems you are likely to encounter on the actual exam. Then when it's time to take the ARE, you will already be comfortable with the format of the exam. Also, comparing your solution with the passing and failing solutions in the book will help you gauge your understanding of the skills covered in the Schematic Design division.

Each sample vignette in this book can be solved directly on the base plan provided or on a sheet of tracing paper. Alternatively, you can download an electronic file of the base plan in PDF format from **www.ppi2pass.com/vignettes** for use in your own CAD program. (On the actual exam, vignettes are solved on the computer using NCARB's own software; see the Introduction for more information about this.) When you are finished with your solution to a vignette, compare it against the sample passing and failing solutions that follow.

While the sample vignettes in this book are intended for you to use as you study for the exam, the practice exam is best used only when you have almost finished your study of the Schematic Design topics. A week or two before you are scheduled to take the division, when you feel you are nearly ready for the exam, do a "dry run" by taking the practice exam in this book. This will hone your test-taking skills and give you a reality check about how prepared you really are.

The experience will be most valuable to you if you treat the practice exam as though it were an actual exam. Do not read the vignettes ahead of time and do not look at the solutions until after you've finished. Try to simulate the exam experience as closely as possible. This means locking yourself away in a quiet space, setting an alarm for the exam's testing time, and working through the entire examination with no coffee, television, or telephone—only your calculator, a pencil, your drafting tools or CAD program, and a few sheets of scratch paper. (On the actual exam, these are provided.) This will help you prepare to budget your time, give you an idea of what the actual exam experience will be like, and help you develop a test-taking strategy that works for you.

The vignettes in the practice exam can be solved the same way as the sample vignettes, either directly on the base plans, on tracing paper, or with a CAD program using the electronic files downloaded from **www.ppi2pass.com/vignettes**. Try to solve each vignette within the target time given. When you are finished, compare your drawing against the passing and failing solutions given in the Solutions section.

The target times for the vignettes in the practice exam are

Interior Layout vignette: 1 hour

Building Layout vignette: 4 hours

When you are finished, compare your solution against the passing and failing solutions given. Then read the solving approach and the list of pitfalls, especially if your own solution looks more like the failing one than the passing one. The explanations will give you a better understanding of the intent of the vignette and why certain choices are right or wrong. If you still are not clear about a particular vignette after reading its solution, review the subject in one of your study resources. Give yourself time for further study, and then try the vignette again.

This book is best used in conjunction with your primary study source or study guide, such as PPI's *ARE Review Manual*. *Schematic Design: ARE Sample Problems and Practice Exam* is not intended to give you all the information you will need to pass this division of the ARE. Rather, it is designed to expose you to the vignette formats and to help you sharpen your problem-solving and test-taking skills. With a sound review and the practice you'll get from this book, you'll be well on your way to successfully passing the Schematic Design division of the Architect Registration Examination.

HOW SI UNITS ARE USED IN THIS BOOK

This book includes equivalent measurements in the text and illustrations using the Système International (SI), or the metric system as it is commonly called. However, the use of SI units for construction and book publishing in the United States is problematic. This is because the building construction industry in the United States (with the exception of federal construction) has generally not adopted the metric system. As a result, equivalent measurements of customary U.S. units (also called English or inch-pound units) are usually given as a *soft* conversion, in which customary U.S. measurements are simply converted into SI units using standard conversion factors. This always results in a number with excessive significant digits. When construction is done using SI units, the building is designed and drawn according to *hard* conversions, where planning dimensions and building products are based on a metric module from the beginning. For example, studs are spaced 400 mm on center to accommodate panel products that are manufactured in standard 1200 mm widths.

During the present time of transition to the Système International in the United States, code-writing bodies, federal laws such as the ADA, product manufacturers, trade associations, and other construction-related industries typically still use the customary U.S. system and make soft conversions to develop SI equivalents. In the case of some product manufacturers, they produce the same product using both measuring systems. Although there are industry standards for developing SI equivalents, there is no perfect consistency for rounding off when conversions are made. For example, the International Building Code shows a 152 mm equivalent when a 6 in dimension is required, while the Americans with Disabilities Act Accessibility Guidelines (ADAAG) give a 150 mm equivalent for the same customary U.S. dimension.

To further complicate matters, each book publisher may employ a slightly different house style in handling SI equivalents when customary U.S. units are used as the primary measuring system. The confusion is likely to continue until the United States construction industry adopts the SI system completely, eliminating the need for dual dimensioning in publishing.

For the purposes of this book, the following conventions have been adopted.

Throughout the book, the customary U.S. measurements are given first with the SI equivalent shown in parentheses. When the measurement is millimeters, units are not shown. For example, a dimension may be indicated as 4 ft 8 in (1422). When the SI equivalent is some other unit, such as for volume or area, the units are indicated. For example, 250 ft^2 (23 m^2).

Following standard conventions, all SI distance measurements in illustrations are in millimeters unless specifically indicated as meters.

When a measurement is given as part of a problem scenario, the SI measurement is not necessarily meant to be roughly equal to the U.S. measurement. For example, a hypothetical force on a beam might be given as 12 kips (12 kN). 12 kips is actually equal to about 53.38 kN, but the intention in such cases is only to provide two problems, one in U.S. units and one in SI units, of about the same difficulty. Solve the entire problem in either U.S. or SI units; don't try to convert from one to the other in the middle of solving a problem.

When dimensions are for informational use, the SI equivalent rounded to the nearest millimeter is used.

When dimensions are given and they relate to planning or design guidelines, the SI equivalent is rounded to the nearest 5 mm for numbers over a few inches and to the nearest 10 mm for numbers over a few feet. When the dimension exceeds several feet, the number is rounded to the nearest 100 mm. For example, if you need a space about 10 ft wide for a given activity, the modular, rounded SI equivalent will be given as 3000 mm. More exact conversions are not required.

When an item is only manufactured to a customary U.S. measurement, the nearest SI equivalent rounded to the nearest millimeter is given, unless the dimension is very small (as for metal gages), in which case a more precise decimal equivalent will be given. Some materials, such as glass, are often manufactured to SI sizes. So, for example, a nominal $^1/_2$ in thick piece of glass will have an SI equivalent of 13 mm but can be ordered as 12 mm.

When there is a hard conversion in the industry and an SI equivalent item is manufactured, the hard conversion is given. For example, a 24 $\times$ 24 ceiling tile would have the hard conversion of 600 $\times$ 600 (instead of 610) because these are manufactured and available in the United States.

When an SI conversion is used by a code agency, such as the International Building Code (IBC), or published in another regulation, such as the ADA Accessibility Guidelines, the SI equivalents used by the issuing agency are printed in this book. For example, the same 10 ft dimension given previously as 3000 mm for a planning guideline would have an SI equivalent of 3048 mm in the context of the IBC because this is what that code requires. The ADA Accessibility Guidelines generally follow the rounding rule, to take SI dimensions to the nearest 10 mm. For example, a 10 ft requirement for accessibility will be shown as 3050 mm. The code requirements for readers outside the United States may be slightly different.

This book uses different abbreviations for pounds of force and pounds of mass in customary U.S. units. The abbreviation used for pounds of force (pounds-force) is lbf, and the abbreviation used for pounds of mass (pounds-mass) is lbm.

RECOMMENDED READING

General Reference

Access Board. *ADAAG Manual: A Guide to the Americans with Disabilities Accessibility Guidelines*. East Providence, RI: BNI Building News.

_____. *ADAAG Manual: Americans with Disabilities Act Accessibility Guidelines for Buildings and Facilities*. Washington, DC: U.S. Architectural and Transportation Barriers Compliance Board. www.access-board.gov/adaag/html/adaag.htm.

ARCOM. *MASTERSPEC*. Salt Lake City: ARCOM. (Familiarity with the format and language of specifications is very helpful.)

ARCOM and American Institute of Architects. *The Graphic Standards Guide to Architectural Finishes: Using Masterspec® to Evaluate, Select, and Specify Materials*. New York: John Wiley & Sons.

Ballast, David Kent, and Steven E. O'Hara. *ARE Review Manual*. Belmont, CA: PPI.

Canadian Commission on Building and Fire Codes. *National Building Code of Canada*. Ottawa: National Research Council of Canada.

Fitch, James Marston. *Historic Preservation: Curatorial Management of the Built World*. Charlottesville: University Press of Virginia.

Guthrie, Pat. *Architect's Portable Handbook*. New York: McGraw-Hill.

Harris, Cyril M., ed. *Dictionary of Architecture and Construction*. New York: McGraw-Hill.

International Code Council. *International Building Code*. Washington, DC: International Code Council.

_____. *Standard on Accessible and Usable Buildings and Facilities* (ICC/ANSI A117.1). Washington, DC: American National Standards Institute, International Code Council.

Patterson, Terry L. *Illustrated 2000 Building Code Handbook*. New York: McGraw-Hill.

Ramsey, Charles G., and Harold R. Sleeper. *Architectural Graphic Standards*. New York: John Wiley & Sons. (The student edition is an acceptable substitute for the professional version.)

U.S. Green Building Council. *LEED Reference Package for New Construction and Major Renovations*. Washington, DC: U.S. Green Building Council.

Schematic Design

Allen, Edward, and Joseph Iano. *The Architect's Studio Companion: Rules of Thumb for Preliminary Design*. New York: John Wiley & Sons.

Ambrose, James, and Peter Brandow. *Simplified Site Design*. New York: John Wiley & Sons.

Ching, Francis D. K., and Steven R. Winkel. *Building Codes Illustrated: A Guide to Understanding the International Building Code*. New York: John Wiley & Sons.

Hoke, John Ray, ed. *Architectural Graphic Standards*. New York: John Wiley & Sons.

Karlen, Mark. *Space Planning Basics*. New York: John Wiley & Sons.

Parker, Harry, John W. MacGuire, and James Ambrose. *Simplified Site Engineering*. New York: John Wiley & Sons.

SAMPLE PROBLEMS

BUILDING LAYOUT 1

Directions

Develop both first- and second-level floor plans for a small two-story building, using the site plans provided. The schematic design must be responsive to the given program and code requirements, and should reflect principles of sound design logic. Adequate and code-compliant circulation should be provided and the orientation of the building on the site must be responsive to site influences.

Develop the floor plans by sizing and locating all required spaces and any corridors. Indicate partition locations, corridors as required, doors, and windows. Label the upper story of the two-story space with the tag "OB" (open to below). (On the actual exam, an included label must be used to indicate this space on the second-floor plan.) Label each space with the tag abbreviation included in the program.

Before beginning, review the program, code information, and the site plan.

Program

A midwestern city is constructing a neighborhood community center. The center will be used primarily as a meeting site and for organized activities for children, teens, and seniors.

1. The center is in a residential area adjacent to a small park to the north of the site. Parking is across the street to the east, so the main entrance must be on the east portion of the site.

2. The major views are to the north and south.

3. The kitchen must have access to service from the alley on the west and direct access to the corridor.

4. The kitchen must be adjacent to the main activity room.

5. The main activity room must have a finished ceiling height of 14 ft (4300). All other spaces shall have a 9 ft (2700) finished ceiling height.

6. The meeting room on the second floor must be capable of being divided into two smaller rooms with a movable partition; when partitioned, each subdivided room must have a separate entrance.

7. Egress may be in any direction.

8. The area of each space shall be within 10% of the required program area.

9. The total corridor area shall not exceed 25% of the total program area.

10. The second-floor envelope must be congruent with or wholly contained within the first-floor envelope, except that doors to the exterior may be recessed for weather protection.

Space Requirements

tag	name	area (ft²)	area (m²)	requirements
RL	reception area/lobby	400	40	Main entrance connects to reception/lobby. Exterior window required.
MA	main activity room	1000	100	Exterior window required. 14 ft (4300) ceilings. Label second floor area "OB".
SA	senior activity room	600	60	Adjacent to reception area. Exterior window required.
K	kitchen	300	30	Immediately adjacent to main activity room.
AS	activity storage room	100	10	Must open onto main activity room.
T	toilet rooms	800	80	Two per floor at 200 ft² (20 m²) each.
ST	stairs	640	64	Two per floor at 160 ft² (16 m²) per stair.
E	elevator shaft	140	14	One per floor at 70 ft² (7 m²). Min. dimension 7 ft (2.1 m).
EE	elevator equipment room	70	7	Adjacent to elevator shaft.
EM	electrical/mechanical room	300	30	
J	janitor's closet, first floor	50	5	
C	coat closet	50	5	Adjacent to lobby.
O	offices	600	60	Four at 150 ft² (15 m²) on second floor. Exterior window required.
MR	meeting room	600	60	Second floor. Exterior window required.
J	janitor's closet, second floor	30	3	
	TOTAL PROGRAM AREA	5680	568	

Code Requirements

Comply with the following code requirements. These are the only code-related criteria required.

Exits

1. Two exits are required from each floor, separated by at least half the maximum overall diagonal distance of the floor.

2. Two exits are required in the main activity room and senior activity room. They must be separated by a minimum of half the maximum overall diagonal distance of the room. Exit doors may discharge directly to the exterior of the building at grade.

3. Every room must connect directly to a corridor or circulation area. Exceptions are elevator equipment rooms, activity storage rooms, and rooms with an area of 50 ft² (5 m²) or less, which may connect to a corridor or circulation area through an intervening space.

4. Exit doors must swing in the direction of travel.

5. Door swings cannot reduce the minimum clear exit path to less than 36 in (915).

Corridors

1. Discharge corridors directly to the exterior at grade or through stairs or circulation areas.

2. The minimum width of corridors is 6 ft (1830).

3. The maximum dead-end corridor length is 20 ft (6100).

4. Do not interrupt corridors with intervening rooms. Circulation areas are not considered to be intervening rooms.

Stairs

1. Discharge stairs directly to the exterior at grade.

2. The minimum width of stairs is 4 ft (1220).

3. Connect stairs directly to a corridor or circulation area at each floor.

Tips

- When reading the directions and program, be sure to scroll down to see all the information.

- Read the program and space requirements carefully.

- On the actual exam, as a space is drawn, dimensions are given on the computer screen. Note that these dimensions are from wall centerline to wall centerline. Take this into consideration when drawing corridors to code-required widths, which are measured from one edge of the corridor to the other.

- While working on one floor, keep the layers from the other floor turned on to help see the limits of the building.

- Use the *check* icon on the screen to check for overlaps while working.

- If one of two overlapping elements cannot be selected, keep clicking without moving the mouse until the desired element is highlighted.

- It is not necessary to show doors or openings in elevator walls.

- Draw each space to approximate size, then arrange the spaces and later adjust the sizes as necessary.

Warnings

- Wall openings may be drawn only between circulation areas, which include corridors. On the actual exam, circulation areas are indicated by a lighter hatched background. Make sure adjacent circulation areas are opened by wall openings or doors.

- Elements cannot be moved from one floor to another.

Tools

Useful tools include the following.

- *zoom* tool for checking clearances and overlapping walls

- *sketch grid* tool to help align elements

- full-screen cursor to help line up walls or other elements

Target Time: 4 hours

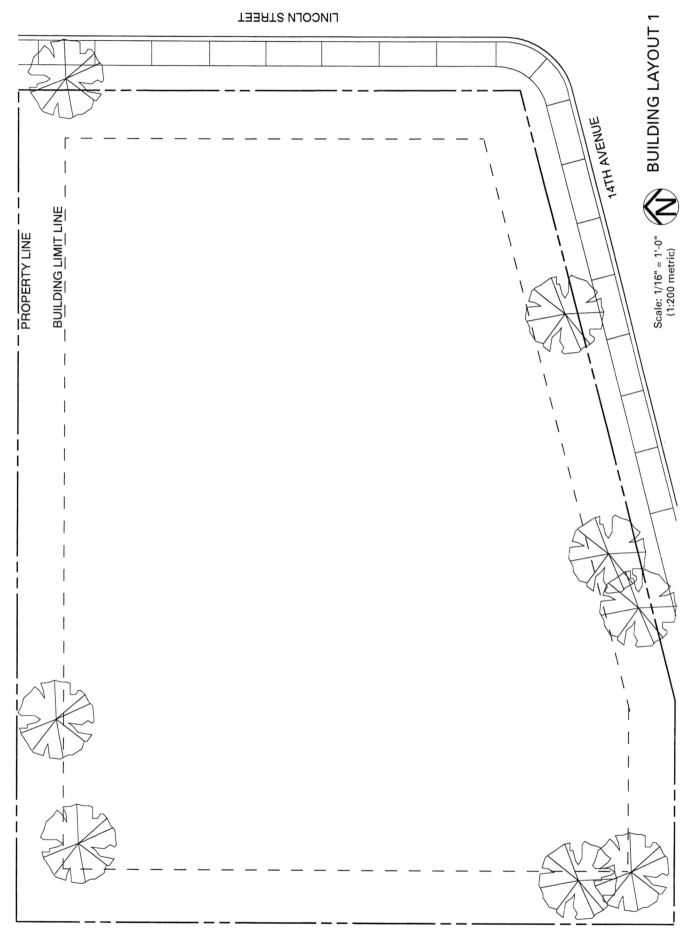

LINCOLN STREET

BUILDING LAYOUT 1

14TH AVENUE

Scale: 1/16" = 1'-0"
(1:200 metric)

PROPERTY LINE

BUILDING LIMIT LINE

BUILDING LAYOUT 1: PASSING SOLUTION

In this good solution the building has been oriented on the site to satisfy all program requirements. The organization of both first- and second-floor plans is logical and direct. All spaces are included and are within the areas stipulated by the program. All exiting requirements have been satisfied.

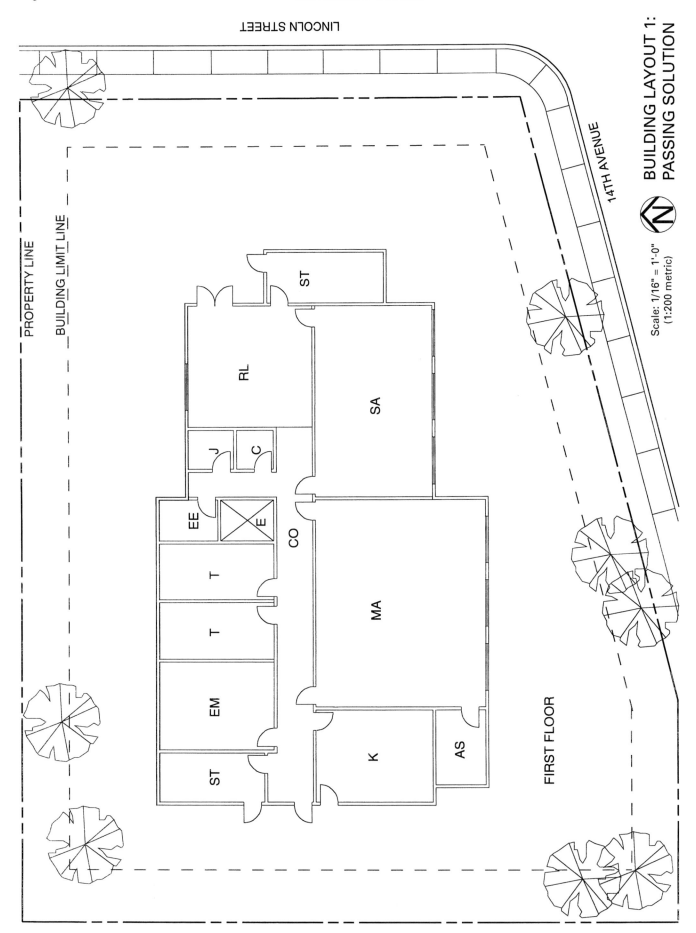

BUILDING LAYOUT 1:
PASSING SOLUTION

Scale: 1/16" = 1'-0"
(1:200 metric)

LINCOLN STREET

PROPERTY LINE

BUILDING LIMIT LINE

14TH AVENUE

FIRST FLOOR

ST

RL

SA

J

C

EE

E

CO

T

T

MA

EM

K

ST

AS

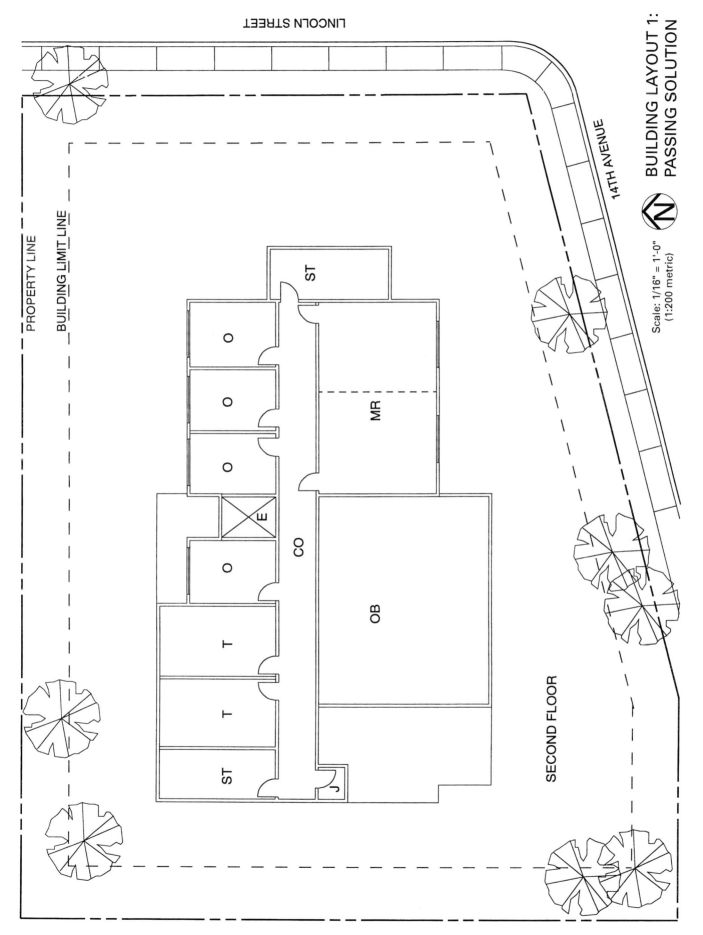

LINCOLN STREET

14TH AVENUE

PROPERTY LINE

BUILDING LIMIT LINE

ST

O

O

O

O

E

T

T

T

ST

J

CO

MR

OB

SECOND FLOOR

BUILDING LAYOUT 1:
PASSING SOLUTION

N

Scale: 1/16" = 1'-0"
(1:200 metric)

BUILDING LAYOUT 1:
FAILING SOLUTION

The general organization of this poor solution is awkward and results in several violations of the program. On the first floor there is no door from the kitchen to the corridor. The width of the corridor to the toilet rooms is less than the 6 ft (1830) required by the program. There is also a major exiting mistake: the two doors from the senior activity room are too close to each other and they swing in.

On the second floor the layout of the offices is not logical. This could be considered a minor problem, but a more significant problem is that one office is too large and two offices are too small. The large office also lacks a window. The second-floor meeting room can be divided by a partition, as the program requires, but the two smaller rooms do not have the required separate entrances.

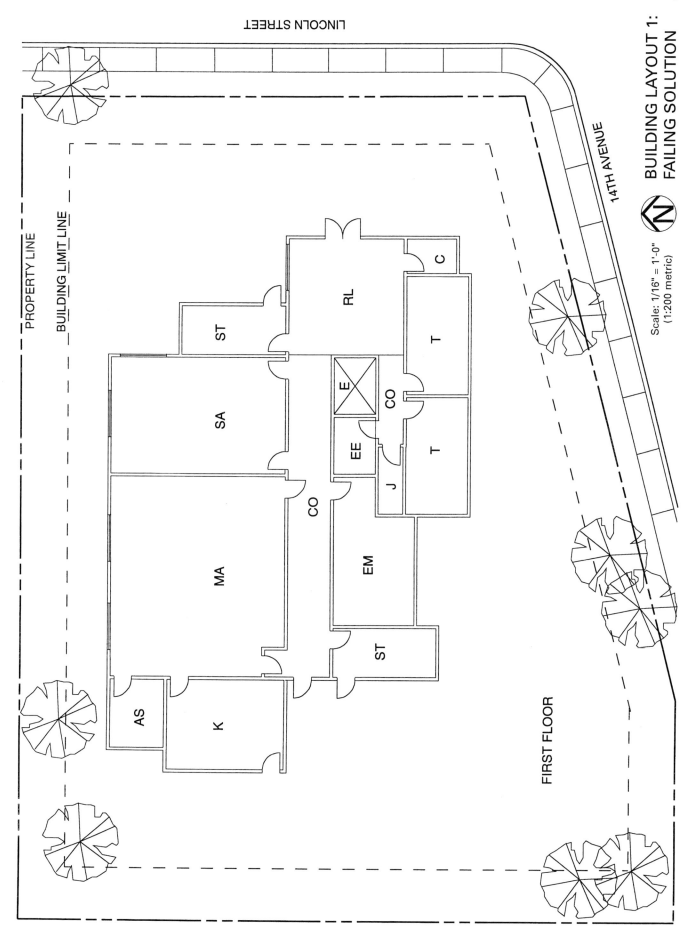

LINCOLN STREET

PROPERTY LINE

BUILDING LIMIT LINE

14TH AVENUE

BUILDING LAYOUT 1:
FAILING SOLUTION

Scale: 1/16" = 1'-0"
(1:200 metric)

FIRST FLOOR

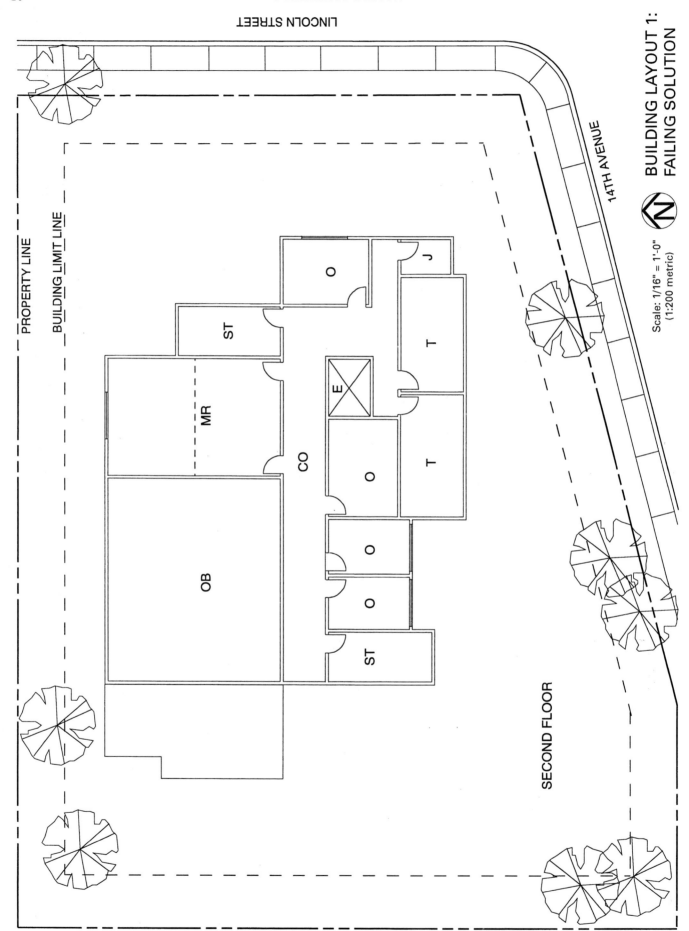

BUILDING LAYOUT 1:
FAILING SOLUTION

Scale: 1/16" = 1'-0"
(1:200 metric)

SECOND FLOOR

BUILDING LAYOUT 2

Directions

Develop both first- and second-level floor plans for a small two-story building, using the site plans provided. The schematic design must be responsive to the given program and code requirements, and should reflect principles of sound design logic. Adequate and code-compliant circulation should be provided and the orientation of the building on the site must be responsive to site influences.

Develop the floor plans by sizing and locating all required spaces and any corridors. Indicate partition locations, corridors as required, doors, and windows. Label the upper story of the two-story space with the tag "OB" (open to below). (On the actual exam, an included label must be used to indicate this space on the second-floor plan.) Label each space with the tag abbreviation included in the program.

Before beginning, review the program, code information, and the site plan.

Program

A large West Coast city is planning a new building to house several neighborhood groups that have formed the Central Neighborhoods Coalition. The goal is to make more efficient use of available funds by consolidating space needs into one structure. The building will contain offices as well as public meeting rooms, conference rooms, and other support facilities.

1. The site is located to the south of a small neighborhood park. Thus, the major view is to the north.

2. Parking is available off site.

3. The main entrance must be from the south along 15th Avenue.

4. All spaces will have a 9 ft (2700) ceiling height except the main meeting room, which will have a 16 ft (4800) ceiling height.

5. The area of each space must be within 10% of the required program area.

6. The total corridor area must not exceed 25% of the total program area.

7. The reception area must have visual control of the lobby, be adjacent to the facility coordinator's office, and have direct access to the facility coordinator's office.

8. The second-floor envelope must be congruent with the first-floor envelope or wholly contained within it, except that first-floor doors leading to the exterior may be recessed for weather protection.

Space Requirements

tag	name	area (ft²)	(m²)	requirements
L	lobby	400	40	At main entrance.
ST	stairs	800	80	Two per floor at 200 ft² (20 m²) per stair.
E	elevator	200	20	One per floor at 100 ft² (10 m²). Minimum dimension: 8 ft (2400).
EE	elevator equipment room	100	10	
R	reception area	150	15	Adjacent to lobby.
FC	facility coordinator's office	200	20	Direct access to reception.
AC	assistant coordinator's office	150	15	Adjacent to facility coordinator.
S	storage room	200	20	Exterior windows prohibited.
MR	meeting room	2000	185	Exterior window with view required. 16 ft (4570) ceiling, two exits, first floor. Label second-floor area "OB".
MS	meeting storage	500	50	Direct access to meeting room. Exterior windows prohibited.
SM	small meeting room	400	40	Exterior window with view required.
T	toilet rooms	600	60	Two per floor at 150 ft² (15 m²) each.
ME	mechanical/electrical room	400	40	
J	janitor's closets	200	20	One per floor at 100 ft² (10 m²) each.
NO	neighborhood director's office	150	15	Direct access to secretarial office. Exterior window required.
CM	community relations office	200	20	Direct access to secretarial office. Exterior window required.
SO	secretarial office	300	30	Exterior window required. Near conference rooms.
W	workroom	150	15	Exterior window prohibited.
B	break room	300	30	
CR	conference rooms	800	80	Two at 400 ft² (40 m²). Second floor.
	TOTAL PROGRAM AREA	8200	805	

Code Requirements

Comply with the following code requirements. These are the only code-related criteria required.

Exits

1. Two exits are required from each floor, separated by at least half the maximum overall diagonal distance of the floor.

2. Two exits are required in the meeting room. They must be separated by a minimum of half the maximum overall diagonal distance of the room. Exit doors may discharge directly to the exterior of the building at grade.

3. Exit doors must swing in the direction of travel.

4. Door swings cannot reduce the minimum clear exit path to less than 36 in (915).

Corridors

1. The minimum clear width of a corridor is 6 ft (1830).

2. The maximum dead-end corridor length is 20 ft (6100).

3. Stairs must discharge directly to the exterior at grade.

4. Every room must connect directly to a corridor or circulation area. Exceptions are the facility coordinator's office and the meeting storage, each of which may connect to a corridor or circulation area through an intervening space. Corridors cannot be interrupted with intervening rooms. However, circulation areas are not considered to be intervening rooms.

Stairs

1. Connect stairs directly to a corridor or circulation area at each floor.

2. The minimum width of stairs is 4 ft (1220).

Tips

- When reading the directions and program, be sure to scroll down to see all the information.

- Read the program and space requirements carefully.

- On the actual exam, as a space is drawn, dimensions are given on the computer screen. Note that these dimensions are from wall centerline to wall centerline. Take this into consideration when drawing corridors to code-required widths, which are measured from one edge of the corridor to the other.

- While working on one floor, keep the layers from the other floor turned on to help see the limits of the building.

- Use the *check* icon on the screen to check for overlaps while working.

- If one of two overlapping elements cannot be selected, keep clicking without moving the mouse until the desired element is highlighted.

- It is not necessary to show doors or openings in elevator walls.

- Draw each space to approximate size, then arrange the spaces and later adjust the sizes as necessary.

Warnings

- Wall openings may be drawn only between circulation areas, which include corridors. On the actual exam, circulation areas are indicated by a lighter hatched background. Make sure adjacent circulation areas are opened by wall openings or doors.

- Elements cannot be moved from one floor to another.

Tools

Useful tools include the following.

- *zoom* tool for checking clearances and overlapping walls

- *sketch grid* tool to help align elements

- full-screen cursor to help line up walls or other elements

Target Time: 4 hours

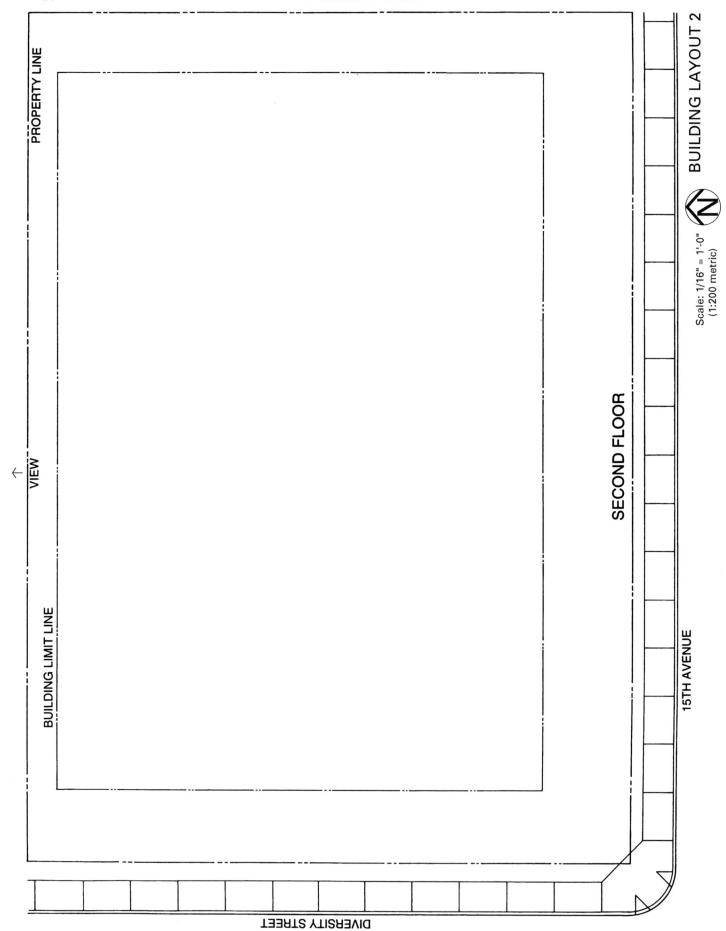

PROPERTY LINE

VIEW

BUILDING LIMIT LINE

SECOND FLOOR

DIVERSITY STREET

15TH AVENUE

BUILDING LAYOUT 2

Scale: 1/16" = 1'-0"
(1:200 metric)

BUILDING LAYOUT 2: PASSING SOLUTION

The solution shown is a very good approach to the problem. All programmed spaces are shown and each is on the level required or on a level that can be reasonably inferred. All programmed spaces, as well as the building as a whole, are within the required size allowances.

The required relationships are all satisfied. The reception area is adjacent to and has visual control of the lobby, and the facility coordinator's office is adjacent to the reception area with direct access. On the second level both the neighborhood director's office and the community relations office have direct access to the secretarial office, which is also near the conference rooms as required.

Design Logic

The organization of the building is direct and very efficient, providing easy access to all spaces. All the public spaces, as well as the elevator on the first floor, are near the entrance. The meeting room and the small meeting room have the required views to the north, and the entrance is properly located. The size of the site makes it possible to lay out the building using a simple, double-loaded corridor organization system. Identical spaces, such as the toilet rooms and janitor's closets, are located in the same position on both the first and second floors. The only slightly awkward space is the break room, but given the nature of the space, an L-shaped room would be acceptable.

The large space, the meeting room, is positioned at a corner of the building so that the upper floor does not have to be planned around it. (Note that the upper portion is labeled "OB" as required by the exam.) In this particular problem, the areas of the conference rooms on the second floor are exactly the same as the areas of the small meeting room and the mechanical room, so they could easily be stacked to maintain a congruent exterior wall.

Code Compliance

All code requirements are satisfied. Two exits are remotely located as required, with the exits leading through the stairways. The two required exits in the meeting room are located remotely, with the doors swinging in the direction of travel. There are no dead-end corridors. The corridors are the correct width, and in no case is the width of the corridor reduced. The stairways are wide enough to provide for the minimum width of stairs. The stairways also correctly discharge directly to the exterior at grade.

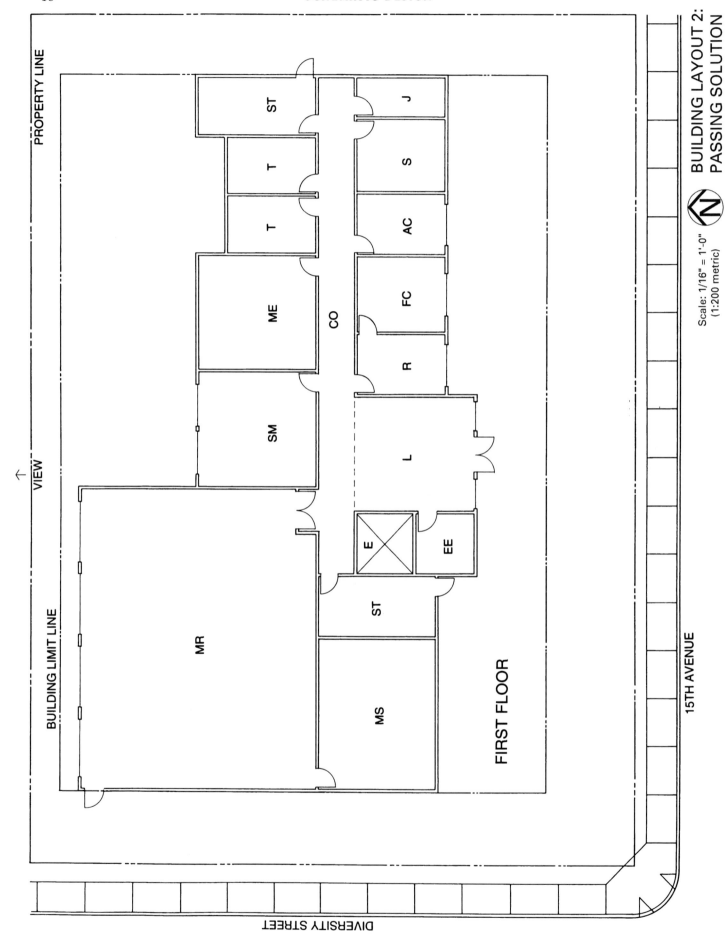

BUILDING LAYOUT 2:
PASSING SOLUTION

Scale: 1/16" = 1'-0"
(1:200 metric)

FIRST FLOOR

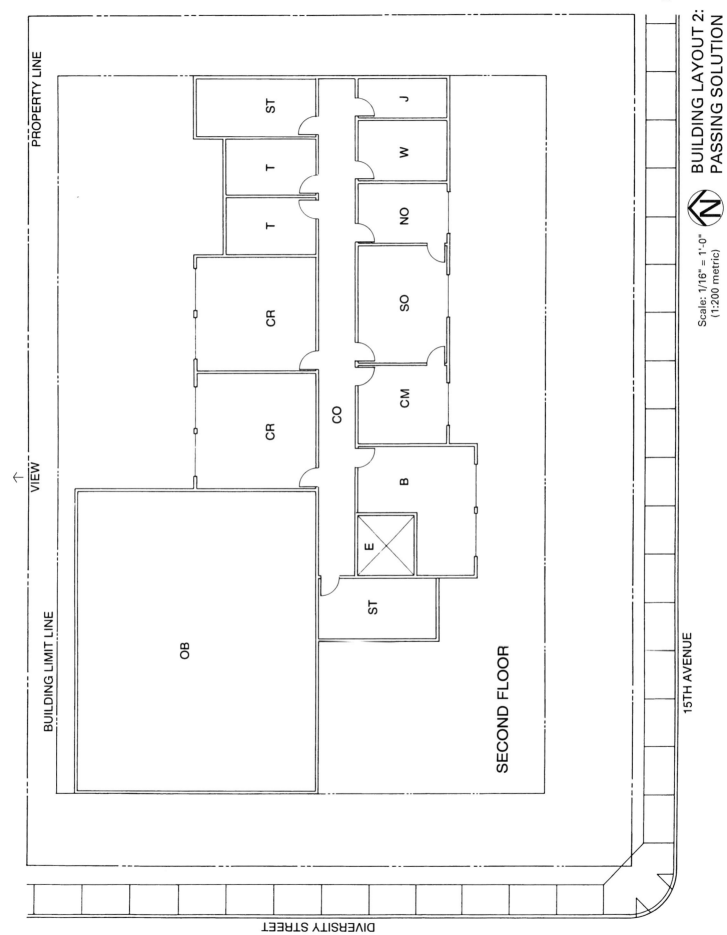

SECOND FLOOR

BUILDING LAYOUT 2:
PASSING SOLUTION

Scale: 1/16" = 1'-0"
(1:200 metric)

BUILDING LAYOUT 2: FAILING SOLUTION

This solution illustrates a poor approach, one that would fail even though the L-shaped corridor system generally works with this plan layout.

Design Logic

All programmed spaces are included, and the overall design logic seems reasonable. An L-shaped corridor system could work, but its implementation here creates some problems. First, a few adjacencies are incorrect. On the first floor the assistant coordinator's office is adjacent to the facility coordinator's office but has no direct access from the corridor. On the second floor there is no direct access to the secretarial office from the neighborhood director's office. Second, the mechanical equipment room is oversized by about 15%, the lobby is undersized to about 68% of its required size, and the assistant coordinator's office is just undersized to 88%, instead of the allowed 90%. Finally, there is a window in the workroom on the second floor when windows are prohibited in this room.

Code Compliance

There are two fatal code problems. On the first floor the required door connecting the corridor with the south stairway is missing and the two exit doors from the meeting room are too close together. Both of these problems could easily have been corrected. Because the code program allows exit doors from the meeting room to open directly to grade, one of the doors could have been moved to the east side of the building.

Possible Corrections

Although not an ideal solution, a door could have been placed between the assistant coordinator's office and the lobby to satisfy the typical requirement that all rooms open directly to a corridor or circulation area. The solution to the second-floor adjacency problem would be more difficult to fix with the existing first-floor configuration. The locations of the secretarial office and the community relations office could be reversed, but the difference in required size of these two offices would make it difficult to lay out simple rectangular offices within the first-floor outline.

It would be difficult to correct the size of the mechanical equipment room unless the assistant coordinator's office was moved to the west of the facility coordinator's office. However, this would create a gap under the classrooms above. This condition illustrates a common problem when rooms are clustered two or more deep away from a corridor, as is the case for the assistant coordinator's office. Even with an L-shaped plan, try to locate all rooms directly adjacent to a corridor or circulation space.

The undersized lobby problem could be corrected simply by drawing the lobby to the wall next to the meeting room and using corridors on each end, creating the same configuration as shown in the plan.

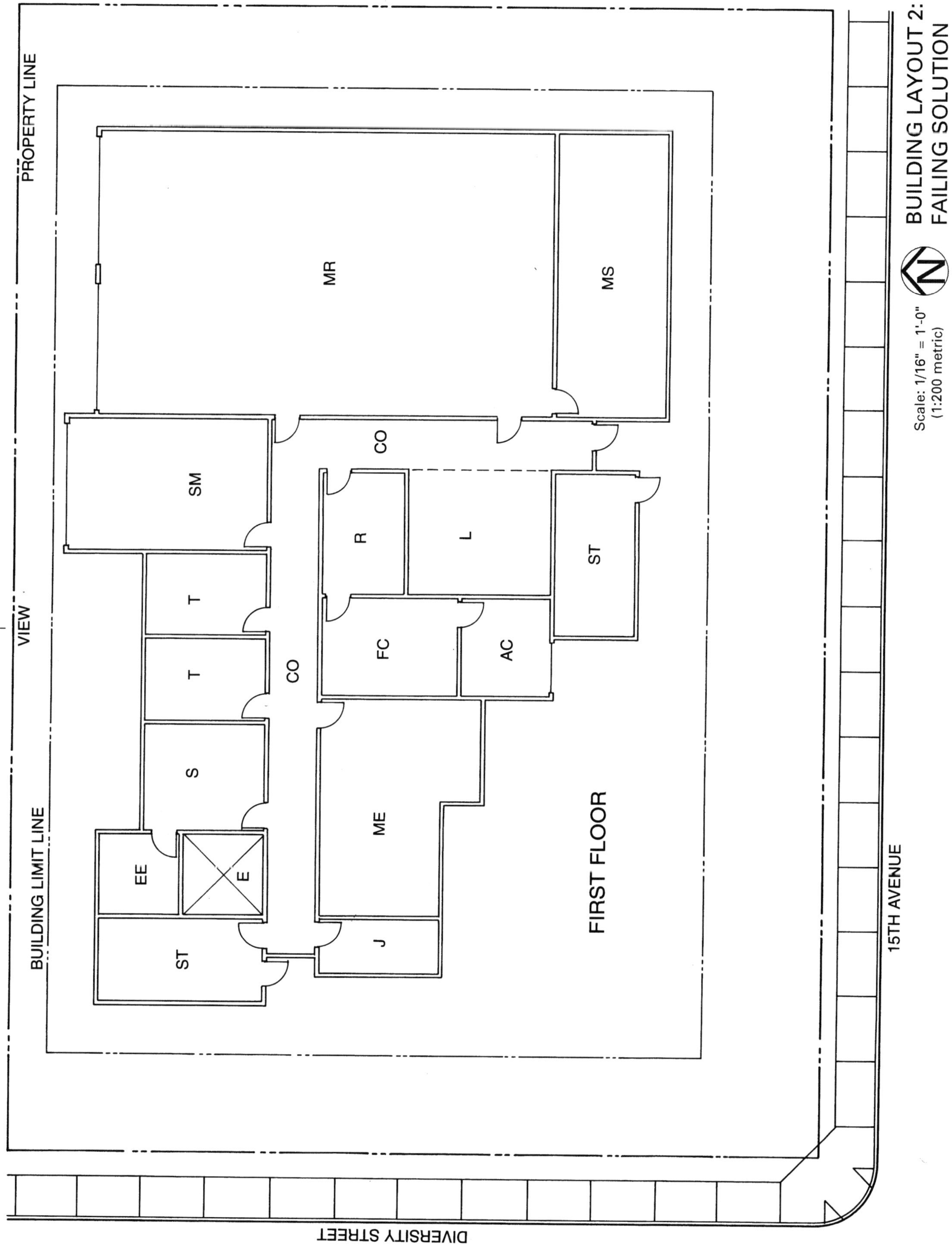

BUILDING LAYOUT 2: FAILING SOLUTION

Scale: 1/16" = 1'-0"
(1:200 metric)

N

PROPERTY LINE

BUILDING LIMIT LINE

VIEW

MR

MS

SM

CO

T

T

S

R

L

ST

FC

AC

CO

CO

EE

E

ME

ST

J

FIRST FLOOR

15TH AVENUE

DIVERSITY STREET

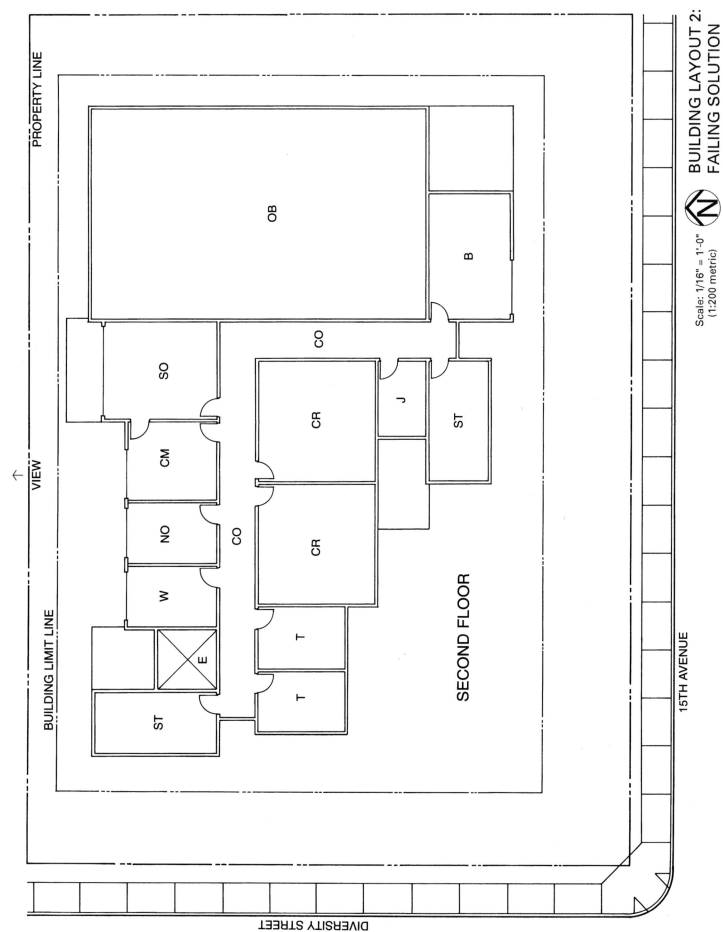

SECOND FLOOR

BUILDING LAYOUT 2: FAILING SOLUTION

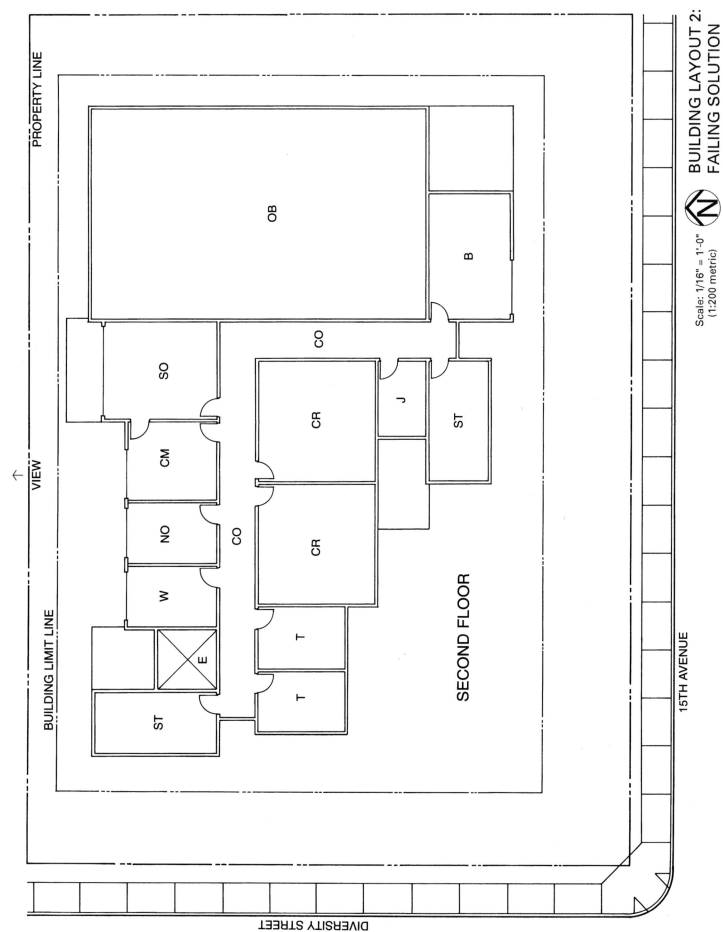

Scale: 1/16" = 1'-0"
(1:200 metric)

15TH AVENUE

INTERIOR LAYOUT 1

Directions

The vacant office space shown in the base plan is to be developed according to the given program and code requirements.

Draw all required spaces using enclosing walls, except for the reception or circulation space which must be defined by exterior walls and/or the walls of the other spaces. Use the appropriate labels indicated in the program to identify each space. Draw doors and place all required furniture.

Before beginning, review the program, code information, and the plan of the vacant office space.

Program

A small management company has leased space in an existing building. The space is approximately 1470 ft² (137 m²) with three windows as shown on the floor plan provided. Develop a space plan and furniture layout that meets the program and code requirements listed here.

1. All spaces and workstations must comply with the accessibility requirements given in the code requirements, including the clear space for a wheelchair to make a 180° turn.

2. The furniture layout must allow for reasonable clearances and access to all the furniture elements. A continuous path that meets the minimum clear distance requirement of the code must be provided to each worktable and to the seating area behind each desk. All furniture listed in the space and furniture requirements must be placed.

3. Label all spaces, including the reception space. The abbreviations given in parentheses may be used. (On the actual exam, specific labels must be used.)

4. The furniture to be placed is shown in the diagram.

Space and Furniture Requirements

1. Reception area (RA)

1	secretarial desk with chair
4	lounge chairs
1	round coffee table
1	large bookcase
1	display rack

2. Manager's office (MO)

   The manager's office must have direct access to the conference room.

1	executive desk with chair
1	credenza
2	side chairs
2	lateral file cabinets
1	large bookcase

3. Agents' offices (AO)—two agent's offices are required

1	executive desk with chair
1	credenza
2	side chairs
1	small bookcase
1	lateral file cabinet

4. Conference room (CR)

1	conference table with chairs
1	credenza

5. Workroom (WR)

1	copy machine
1	worktable
3	lateral file cabinet

(On the actual exam, pre-drawn furniture is available under the *draw* icon.)

Code Requirements

1. The space required for a wheelchair to make a 180° turn is a clear space of 60 in (1525) in diameter.

2. The minimum clear distance between walls or between a wall and any other obstruction along an aisle or corridor shall be 36 in (914).

3. Doorways must have a clear opening of 32 in (813) when the door is open 90°, measured between the face of the door and the opposite stop.

4. Minimum maneuvering clearances at doors shall be as shown on the accompanying illustration.

5. If a doorway has two independently operated door leaves, at least one leaf shall meet the requirements above for clear width and maneuvering clearances.

Tips

- When reading the directions and program, be sure to scroll down to see all the information.

- Check for overlaps while working by using the *check* tool.

- If clicking on an element doesn't select it because other elements are overlapping, keep clicking without moving the mouse until the desired element highlights.

Warnings

- Doors cannot be attached to existing walls. They can only be attached to walls drawn for the rooms.

Tools

Useful tools include the following.

- *zoom* tool for laying out furniture within individual rooms and for checking clearances and overlapping walls

- *sketch circle* tool for checking accessibility turnaround space, clearance between furniture and walls, and maneuvering space at doors

- *sketch grid* tool to make the approximate size and scale of rooms easier to see

Target Time: 1 hour

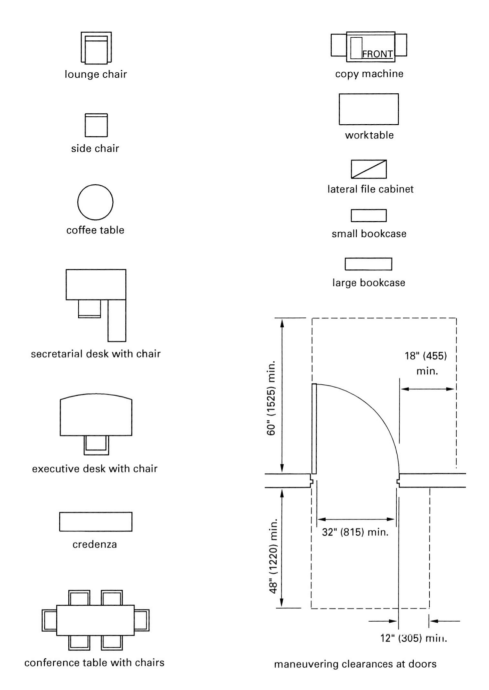

lounge chair

side chair

coffee table

secretarial desk with chair

executive desk with chair

credenza

conference table with chairs

copy machine

FRONT

worktable

lateral file cabinet

small bookcase

large bookcase

60" (1525) min.

18" (455) min.

48" (1220) min.

32" (815) min.

12" (305) min.

maneuvering clearances at doors

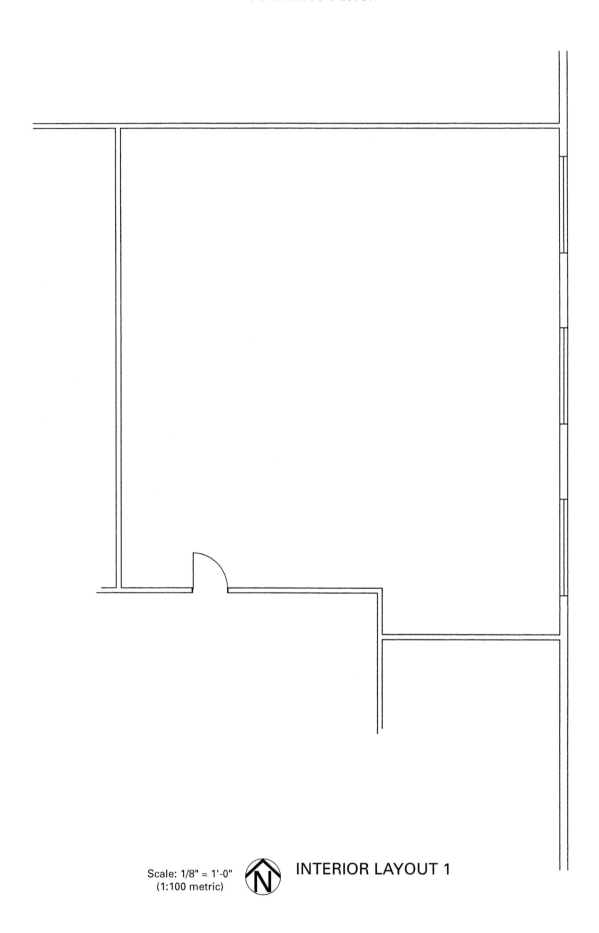

Scale: 1/8" = 1'-0"
(1:100 metric)

INTERIOR LAYOUT 1

INTERIOR LAYOUT 1:
PASSING SOLUTION

In this solution all the required spaces are laid out in a logical and efficient manner with sufficient room for all the furniture. Clearances around furniture and maneuvering clearances at doors satisfy accessibility requirements. The only minor problem with this solution is that there is not a full 3 ft (915) space between the executive desk chairs and the credenzas in the two agents' offices. This could easily have been corrected by moving the desk and chair forward.

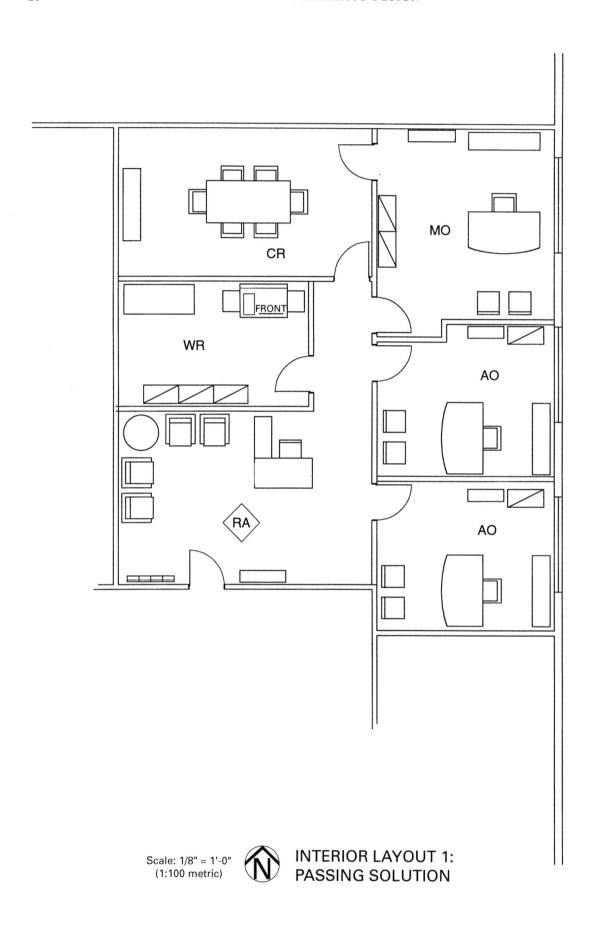

Scale: 1/8" = 1'-0"
(1:100 metric)

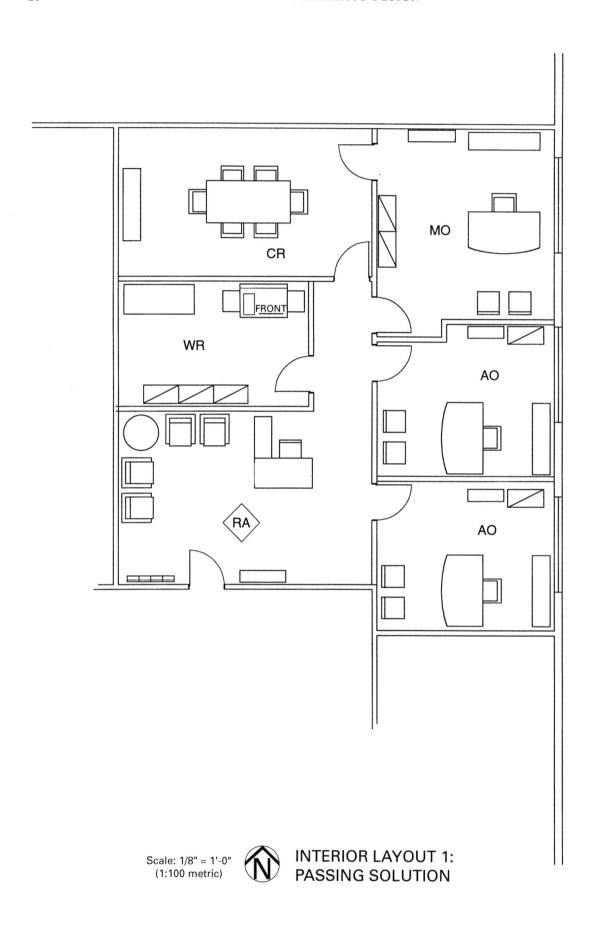

**INTERIOR LAYOUT 1:
PASSING SOLUTION**

INTERIOR LAYOUT 1:
FAILING SOLUTION

This solution violates several program requirements. There is no direct access (doorway) between the manager's office and conference room. There is not enough space for accessibility at the door to the manager's office, the bookcase encroaches into the space inside the office, and there is not enough space on the strike side of the door on the outside of the door. The lounge chairs are too close to the wall of the conference room for accessibility, and the space in the workroom is too tight. Finally, the display rack is missing from the reception area.

PROFESSIONAL PUBLICATIONS, INC.

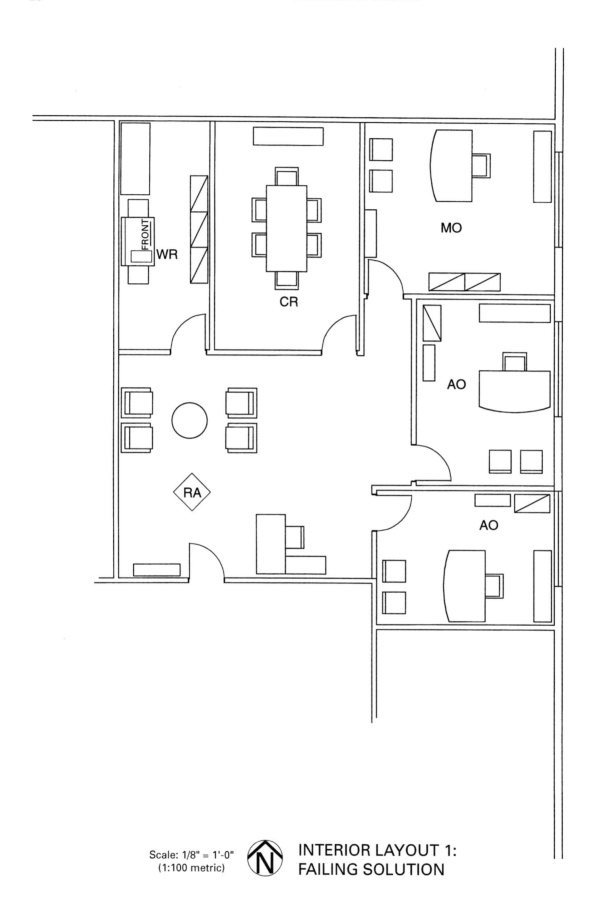

Scale: 1/8" = 1'-0"
(1:100 metric)

**INTERIOR LAYOUT 1:
FAILING SOLUTION**

INTERIOR LAYOUT 2

Directions

The vacant office space shown in the base plan is to be developed according to the following program and code requirements.

Draw all required spaces using enclosing walls, except for the reception or circulation space, which must be defined by exterior walls and/or the walls of the other spaces. Use the labels given in the program in parentheses to identify each space. Draw doors and place all required furniture. Before beginning, review the program, code information, and the plan of the vacant office space.

Program

A college is planning to relocate its admission office to an existing low-rise building. The space is approximately 1700 ft² (160 m²) with windows as shown on the floor plan. Develop a space plan and furniture layout that meets the program and code requirements listed below.

1. All spaces and workstations must comply with the accessibility requirements given in the code requirements, including the clear space for a wheelchair to make a 180° turn.

2. The furniture layout must allow for reasonable clearances and access to all furniture elements. A continuous path that meets the minimum clear distance requirement of the code must be provided to each worktable and to the seating area behind each desk. Place all the furniture listed in the space and furniture requirements.

3. All spaces must be labeled, including the reception space. The abbreviations given in parentheses may be used. (On the actual exam, specific labels must be used.)

4. The furniture to be placed is shown in the diagram.

Space and Furniture Requirements

1. Reception area (RA)

   The configuration and furniture layout of this space must permit a clear view of the suite's main entrance door from the secretarial desk.

   This is the only space to be used for circulation.

   All spaces must have direct access to this space.

   > 1 secretarial desk with chair
   > 3 lounge chairs
   > 1 side table
   > 1 worktable with 1 side chair

   > 1 large bookcase
   > 2 lateral file cabinets

2. Director's office (DO)

   This space must have an exterior window.

   This space must have direct access to the assistant director's office.

   > 1 executive desk with chair
   > 1 credenza
   > 2 side chairs
   > 2 lateral file cabinets
   > 1 large bookcase

3. Assistant director's office (AD)

   This space must have an exterior window.

   This space must have direct access to the director's office.

   > 1 executive desk with chair
   > 1 credenza
   > 2 side chairs
   > 1 small bookcase

4. Admission clerks' office (AC)

   This space must have an exterior window.

   > 2 secretarial desks with chairs
   > 4 lateral file cabinets
   > 1 large bookcase

5. Conference room (CR)

   This space must have an exterior window.

   > 1 conference table with chairs
   > 1 credenza
   > 1 small bookcase

6. File/workroom (FW)

   > 1 copy machine
   > 1 worktable
   > 8 lateral file cabinets

Both right- and left-hand returns can be used for secretarial desks. (On the actual exam, pre-drawn furniture is available under the *draw* icon.)

Code Requirements

1. The space required for a wheelchair to make a 180° turn is a clear space of 60 in (1525) in diameter.

2. The minimum clear distance between walls or between a wall and any other obstruction along an aisle or corridor shall be 36 in (914).

3. Doorways must have a clear opening of 32 in (813) when the door is open 90°, measured between the face of the door and the opposite stop.

4. Minimum maneuvering clearances at doors shall be as shown on the accompanying illustration.

5. If a doorway has two independently operated door leaves, at least one leaf shall meet the requirements above for clear width and maneuvering clearances.

Tips

- When reading the directions and program, be sure to scroll down to see all the information.

- Check for overlaps while working by using the *check* tool.

- If clicking on an element doesn't select it because other elements are overlapping, keep clicking without moving the mouse until the desired element highlights.

Warnings

- Doors cannot be attached to existing walls. They can only be attached to walls drawn for the rooms.

Tools

Useful tools include the following.

- *zoom* tool for laying out furniture within individual rooms and for checking clearances and overlapping walls

- *sketch circle* tool for checking accessibility turnaround space, clearance between furniture and walls, and maneuvering space at doors

- *sketch grid* tool to make the approximate size and scale of rooms easier to see.

Target Time: 1 hour

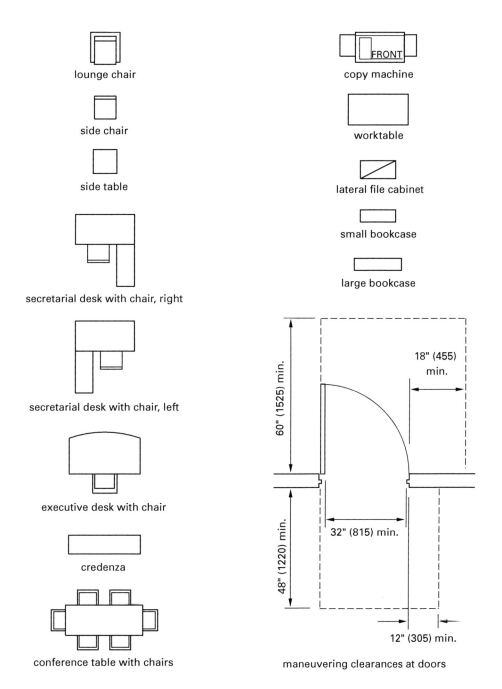

lounge chair

side chair

side table

secretarial desk with chair, right

secretarial desk with chair, left

executive desk with chair

credenza

conference table with chairs

copy machine

worktable

lateral file cabinet

small bookcase

large bookcase

60" (1525) min.

48" (1220) min.

18" (455) min.

32" (815) min.

12" (305) min.

maneuvering clearances at doors

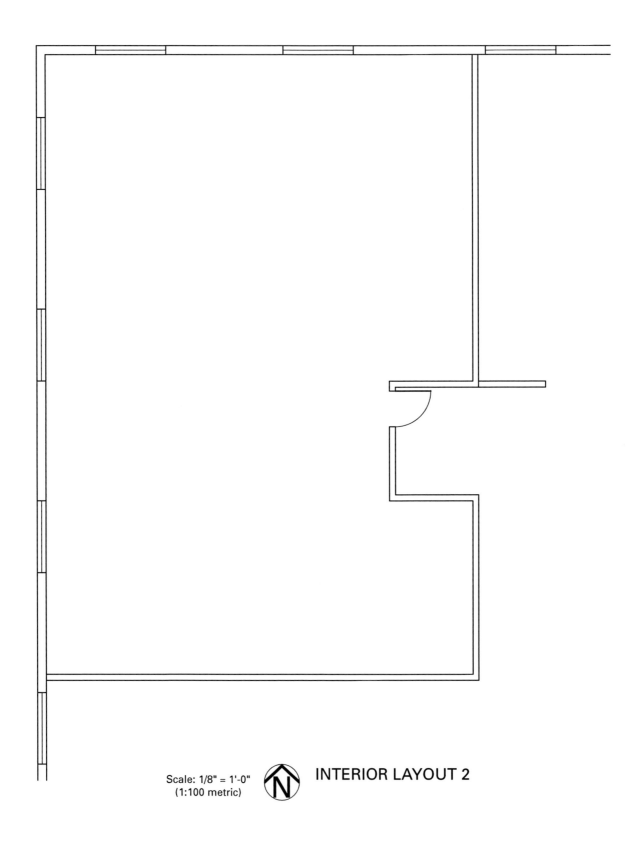

Scale: 1/8" = 1'-0"   **INTERIOR LAYOUT 2**
  (1:100 metric)

INTERIOR LAYOUT 2: PASSING SOLUTION

To solve this vignette, the examinee must set the location of walls that will create the spaces required by the program. The examinee must also place the required furniture in the spaces in such a way that the code requirements are satisfied.

Solving Approach

Step 1 Roughly locate the walls that will define the various spaces required by the program. Most offices and rooms in the Interior Layout vignette will require a minimum width from 12 ft to 14 ft (3.7 m to 4.3 m). The spaces that require windows should be laid out first along the exterior wall. Although the director's office could be anywhere along the exterior wall, the corner position is a good place to start planning.

Step 2 Estimate the most likely position of the other spaces that do not require windows, making sure to leave the reception area with direct access to the entrance door. In this vignette, all spaces except the workroom and reception area require exterior windows. This suggests that the workroom should be in the southeast portion of the plan.

Step 3 The assistant director's office must have direct access to the director's office, so the two rooms must be adjacent. Draw the assistant director's office adjacent to the director's office, estimating the length it will need to be; the exact positions of the walls can be adjusted later as the furniture is placed and it becomes clearer exactly what size space is needed. The placement of the assistant director's office then suggests the locations of the conference room and the admission clerks' office.

Step 4 Draw the remaining room, which is the file/workroom, in the southeast portion of the space. The walls of this room can also be adjusted when the furniture is placed. Place the doors to the rooms.

Step 5 First, place all the required furniture in each space. Then position the furniture in a logical way. Make sure all the code clearances are satisfied, especially the clearance on the pull side of all doors. It is helpful to use sketch circles to verify that all clearances are correct. In order to make all furniture fit with correct clearances, it may be necessary to modify the size of some spaces by moving walls. Make adjustments until all furniture is positioned in accordance with the requirements.

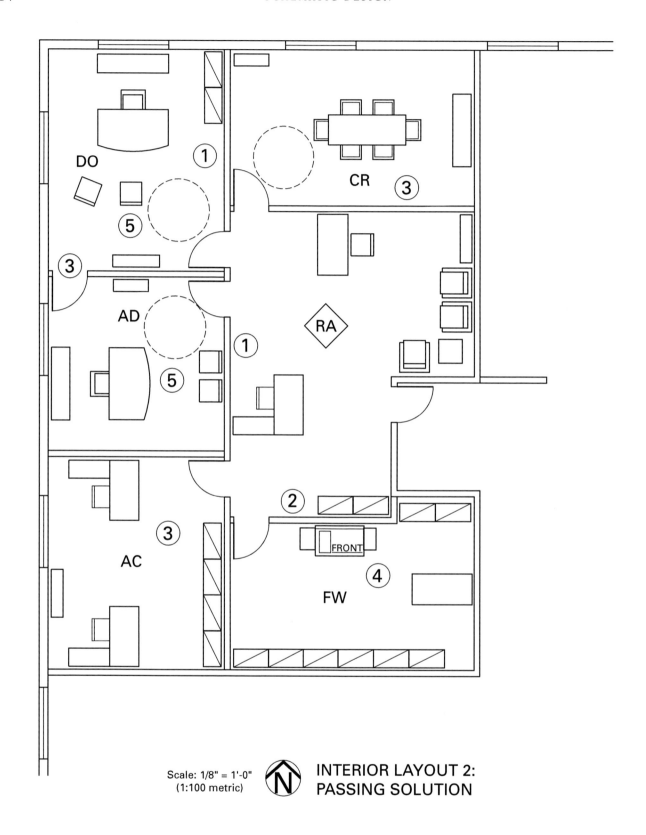

Scale: 1/8" = 1'-0"
(1:100 metric)

**INTERIOR LAYOUT 2:
PASSING SOLUTION**

INTERIOR LAYOUT 2: FAILING SOLUTION

Pitfalls

Note 1 One of the three lounge chairs required in the reception area is missing.

Note 2 There is not enough space for accessibility between one desk and the large bookcase in the clerks' office.

Note 3 There is not enough accessibility clearance in the director's office at the strike side of the door to the assistant director's office; a minimum of 12 in (305) on the push side is required.

Note 4 On the pull side of the same door, there is not enough accessibility clearance for the approach; a minimum of 60 in (1525) is required. The bookcase could have been moved south to allow this.

Note 5 One of the eight lateral files required in the file/workroom is missing.

Note 6 The small bookcase required in the conference room is missing.

Note 7 The conference room does not have a window.

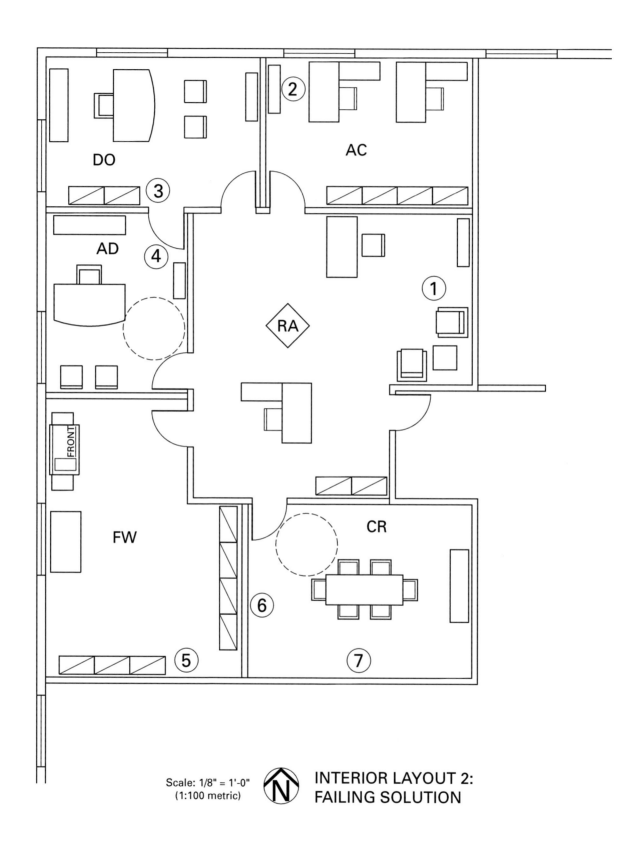

DO

AC

AD

RA

FW

FRONT

CR

Scale: 1/8" = 1'-0"
(1:100 metric)

INTERIOR LAYOUT 2:
FAILING SOLUTION

PRACTICE EXAM

BUILDING LAYOUT

Directions

Develop both first- and second-level floor plans for a small two-story building, using the site plans provided. The schematic design must be responsive to the given program and code requirements, and should reflect principles of sound design logic. Adequate and code-compliant circulation should be provided and the orientation of the building on the site must be responsive to site influences.

Develop the floor plans by sizing and locating all required spaces and any corridors. Indicate partition locations, corridors as required, doors, and windows. Label the upper story of the two-story space with the tag "OB" (open to below). (On the actual exam, an included label must be used to indicate this space on the second-floor plan.) Label each space with the tag abbreviation included in the program.

Before beginning, review the program, code information, and the site plan.

Program

A midsize college is constructing a center for ethnic studies. The building will be used for group meetings and events and will include a specialized resource library.

1. The building is on the college campus adjacent to the main quadrangle, which is to the north of the site. Parking is provided in a nearby parking structure.

2. The major view is to the north, toward the quadrangle.

3. The kitchen must have direct access to the corridor. The kitchen must have an exterior door to provide access to the service road on the south.

4. The reception area is to have visual control of the building entry as well as of the lobby.

5. The main entrance to the building shall be from the north.

6. Egress may be in any direction.

7. Every space shall have a 9 ft (2700) finished ceiling, except for the meeting/activity room, which will have a 15 ft (4600) finished ceiling.

8. Each programmed area shall be within 10% of the required program area.

9. The total corridor area shall not exceed 25% of the total program area.

10. The second-floor envelope must be congruent with or wholly contained within the first-floor envelope, except that doors to the exterior may be recessed for weather protection.

Spaces Requirements

tag	name	area (ft²)	(m²)	requirements
LB	lobby	400	40	Main entrance connects to lobby. Direct access to meeting/activity room.
R	reception area	150	15	Exterior window required. Adjacent to lobby. Near secretarial office.
AO	administrator's office	200	20	Exterior window required. Direct access to secretarial office.
SO	secretarial office	150	15	Exterior window required.
AA	administrative assistant	200	20	Exterior window required. Direct access to secretarial office.
S	storage room	150	15	No exterior windows. Near secretarial and administrator's offices.
MA	meeting/activity room	2400	240	Exterior window and view. 15 ft (4600) ceiling, two exits, first floor. Label second-floor area "OB".
K	kitchen	600	60	Direct access to meeting/activity room. Direct access to corridor. Exterior door for access to service road.
LO	lounge	300	30	Exterior window required. Near lobby.
L	library	900	90	Exterior window required. Second floor. Direct access to head librarian's office.
HO	head librarian's office	200	20	Exterior window required. Direct access to library.
W	library workroom	200	20	Adjacent to librarian's office.
CR	classrooms	600	60	Two at 300 ft² (30 m²) each. Exterior window required. Near seminar room.
SR	seminar room	300	30	Exterior window required. Near library.
ST	stair	800	80	Two per floor at 200 ft² (20 m²) per stair.
E	elevator shaft	200	20	One per floor at 100 ft² (10 m²). Minimum dimension: 7 ft (2100).
EE	elevator equipment room	100	10	Adjacent to elevator shaft on first floor.
T	toilet rooms	600	60	Two per floor at 150 ft² (15 m²) each.
ME	mechanical/electrical room	400	40	First floor. Exterior wall required.
J	janitor's closets	200	20	One per floor at 100 ft² (10 m²) each.
	TOTAL PROGRAM AREA	9050	905	

Code Requirements

Comply with the following code requirements. These are the only code-related criteria required.

Exits

1. Two exits are required from each floor, separated by at least half the maximum overall diagonal distance of the floor.

2. Two exits are required in the meeting/activity room. They must be separated by a minimum of half the maximum overall diagonal distance of the room. Exit doors may discharge directly to the exterior of the building at grade.

3. Every room must connect directly to a corridor or circulation area. Exceptions are the elevator equipment room, the storage room, and any room with an area of 50 ft^2 (5 m^2) or less, which may connect to a corridor or circulation area through an intervening space.

4. Exit doors must swing in the direction of travel. Exterior exit doors may swing across the building limit line.

5. Door swings cannot reduce the minimum clear exit path to less than 36 in (915).

Corridors

1. Corridors must discharge directly to the exterior at grade or through stairs or circulation areas.

2. The minimum width of a corridor is 6 ft (1830).

3. The maximum length of a dead-end corridor is 20 ft (6100).

4. Corridors must not be interrupted by intervening rooms. Circulation areas are not considered intervening rooms.

Stairs

1. Stairs must discharge directly to the exterior at grade.

2. The minimum width of stairs is 4 ft (1220).

3. Stairs must connect directly to a corridor or circulation area at each floor.

Tips

- When reading the directions and program, be sure to scroll down to see all the information.

- Read the program and program spaces carefully.

- On the actual exam, as a space is drawn, dimensions are given on the computer screen. Note that these dimensions are from wall centerline to wall centerline. Take this into consideration when drawing corridors to code-required widths, which are measured from one edge of the corridor to the other.

- While working on one floor, keep the layers from the other floor turned on to help see the limits of the building.

- Use the *check* icon on the screen to check for overlaps while working.

- If one of two overlapping elements cannot be selected, keep clicking without moving the mouse until the desired element is highlighted.

- It is not necessary to show doors or openings in elevator walls.

- Draw each space to approximate size, then arrange the spaces and later adjust the sizes as necessary.

Warnings

- Wall openings may be drawn only between circulation areas, which include corridors. On the actual exam, circulation areas are indicated by a lighter hatched background. Make sure adjacent circulation areas are opened by wall openings or doors.

- Elements cannot be moved from one floor to another.

Tools

Useful tools include the following.

- *zoom* tool for checking clearances and overlapping walls

- *sketch grid* tool to help align elements

- full-screen cursor to help line up walls or other elements

Target Time: 4 hours

↑
VIEW

100' (30 m)

120' (37 m)

PROPERTY LINE

BUILDING LIMIT LINE

FIRST FLOOR

Scale: 1/16" = 1'-0"   **BUILDING LAYOUT**
(1:200 metric)

↑
VIEW
100' (30 m)

120' (37 m)

BUILDING LIMIT LINE

PROPERTY LINE

SECOND FLOOR

Scale: 1/16" = 1'-0"      **BUILDING LAYOUT**
(1:200 metric)

INTERIOR LAYOUT

Directions

The vacant office space shown in the plan is to be developed according to the given program and code requirements.

Draw all required spaces using enclosing walls, except for the reception or circulation space which must be defined by exterior walls and/or the walls of the other spaces. Use the appropriate labels indicated in the program to identify each space. Draw doors and place all required furniture.

Before beginning, review the program, code information, and the plan of the vacant office space.

Program

The DC&H law firm has leased space in an existing mid-rise building. The space is approximately 1200 ft² (110 m²) with two windows as shown on the floor plan. Develop a space plan and furniture layout that meets the program and code requirements listed below.

1. All spaces and workstations must comply with the accessibility requirements given in the code requirements (including the clear space for a wheelchair to make a 180° turn).

2. The furniture layout must allow for reasonable clearances and access to all the furniture elements. A continuous path that meets the minimum clear distance requirement of the code must be provided to each worktable and to the seating area behind each desk. All furniture listed in the space and furniture requirements must be placed.

3. Label all spaces, including the reception space. (On the actual exam, a specific label must be used.)

4. The furniture to be placed is shown in the diagram.

Space and Furniture Requirements

1. Reception area (RA)

   The configuration and furniture layout for this space must allow a clear view of the suite's main entrance door from a secretarial desk.

   This is the only space to be used for circulation.

   All other spaces must have direct access to this space.

       2   secretarial desks with chairs

       4   lounge chairs

       1   side table

       1   large bookcase

       2   lateral file cabinets

2. Partner's office (PO)

   This space must have an exterior window.

   This space must have direct access to the conference room.

       1   executive desk with chair

       1   credenza

       2   side chairs

       2   lateral file cabinets

       1   large bookcase

3. Associate's office (AO)

   This space must have an exterior window.

       1   executive desk with chair

       1   credenza

       2   side chairs

       1   small bookcase

       1   lateral file cabinet

4. Conference room (CR)

       1   conference table with chairs

       1   large bookcase

5. Workroom (WR)

       1   copy machine

       1   worktable

       3   lateral file cabinets

Both right- and left-hand returns can be used for secretarial desks. (On the actual exam, pre-drawn furniture is available under the *draw* icon.)

Code Requirements

1. The space required for a wheelchair to make a 180° turn is a clear space with a diameter of 60 in (1525).

2. The minimum clear distance between walls or between a wall and any other obstruction along an aisle or corridor shall be 36 in (914).

3. A doorway must have a clear opening of 32 in (813) when the door is open 90°, measured between the face of the door and the opposite stop.

4. Minimum maneuvering clearances at doors shall be as shown on accompanying illustration.

5. If a doorway has two independently operated door leaves, at least one leaf shall meet the requirements above for clear width and maneuvering clearances.

Tips

- When reading the directions and program, be sure to scroll down to see all the information.
- Check for overlaps while working by using the *check* icon on the screen.
- If one of two overlapping elements cannot be selected, keep clicking without moving the mouse until the desired element is highlighted.

Warnings

- Doors cannot be attached to existing walls. They can only be attached to walls drawn for the rooms.

Tools

Useful tools include the following.
- *zoom* tool for laying out furniture within individual rooms and for checking clearances and overlapping walls
- *sketch circle* tool for checking accessibility turnaround space, clearance between furniture and walls, and maneuvering space at doors
- *sketch grid* tool to easily see the approximate size and scale of rooms

Target Time: 1 hour

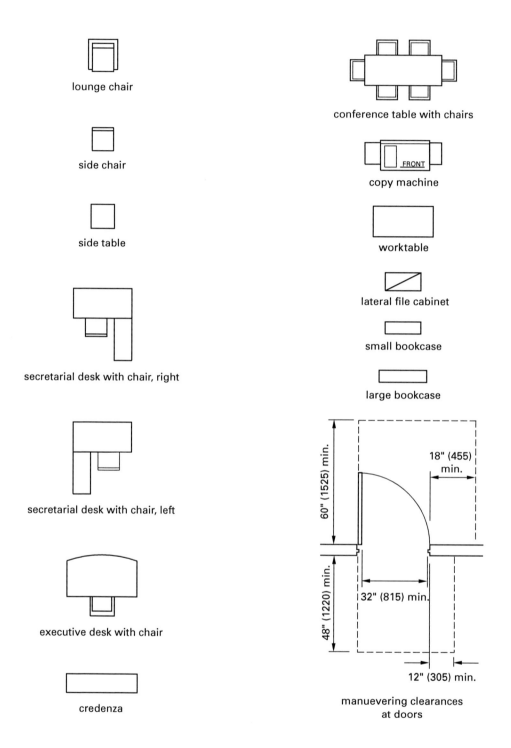

lounge chair

side chair

side table

secretarial desk with chair, right

secretarial desk with chair, left

executive desk with chair

credenza

conference table with chairs

copy machine

worktable

lateral file cabinet

small bookcase

large bookcase

60" (1525) min.

18" (455) min.

48" (1220) min.

32" (815) min.

12" (305) min.

manuevering clearances
at doors

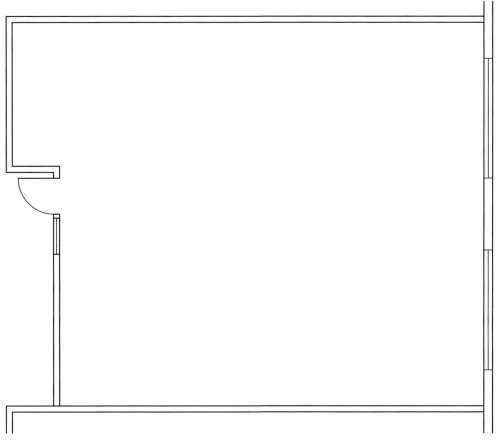

Scale: 1/8" = 1'-0"
(1:100 metric)

INTERIOR LAYOUT

PRACTICE EXAM: SOLUTIONS

BUILDING LAYOUT: PASSING SOLUTION

This vignette requires the examinee to plan spaces for a small two-story building on a given site to meet program parameters while conforming to code requirements.

Solving Approach

Step 1 Because the program is specific about where the entrance must be and what the major view is, the entry can be planned for the north side of the site along with the meeting/activity room, which must have a view and exterior windows.

Step 2 Place the meeting/activity room to one side of the site or the other, leaving room for all the other spaces. Because there will be no second-floor spaces above this large space, the remainder of the first and second floors can be planned almost as a second building, as long as the adjacencies between the meeting/activity room and the lobby and kitchen are maintained.

Step 3 Consider a simple double-loaded corridor organizational scheme for the remainder of the building, with the stairs at both ends of the corridor. Some preliminary room sizing would indicate that the corridor has to be an L-shaped configuration because of the building limit line.

Step 4 Using the adjacency requirements of the program, locate the lobby, reception area, kitchen, and lounge near the main entrance. The elevator should be in this area. Make sure the kitchen opens to the outside so it has access to the service road.

Step 5 Position the stairs at the ends of the corridor. Their exact position can be adjusted when the other spaces are laid out.

Step 6 Because the required areas of the offices are similar and there are specific adjacency requirements, these can be positioned with the same depth and along the west side of the corridor. This gives a wider planning area on the east side of the corridor than on the west. This type of imbalance is often useful when completing a second-floor plan.

Step 7 Block out the mechanical/electrical room and the toilet rooms. With the stair at the building limit line, this suggests that the storage room must be on the west side of the corridor. The janitor room can be placed with the elevator equipment room.

Step 8 On the second floor, use the same corridor configuration. Position the stairs, elevator, and toilet rooms above those on the first floor.

Step 9 Review the program and find the largest area required on the second floor, which is the library. The largest area is frequently the most difficult to position, so do this first. Draw the library with a reasonable aspect ratio.

Step 10 The program requires that the head librarian's office have direct access (a door) to the library and be adjacent to the workroom. This office and the workroom will fit between the library and the toilet rooms.

Step 11 Position the remaining rooms where they will fit and in such a way that exterior windows can be placed.

Step 12 Locate doors as required, making sure that all exit doors swing out and that the stairs are connected correctly to the corridors and exterior.

Step 13 Check for overlaps, correct room sizes, and places where the second floor overhangs the first floor.

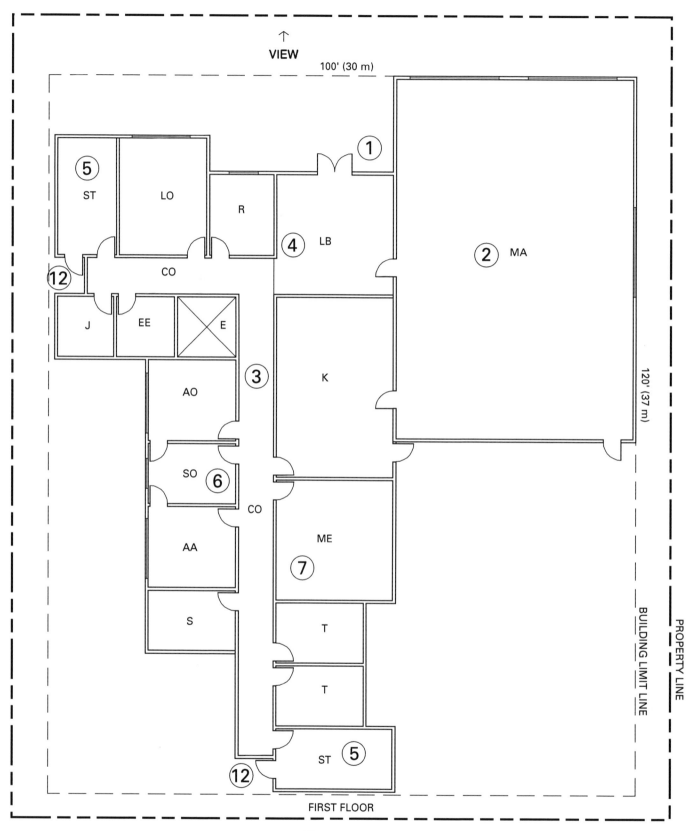

↑
VIEW

100' (30 m)

120' (37 m)

BUILDING LIMIT LINE

PROPERTY LINE

FIRST FLOOR

Scale: 1/16" = 1'-0"
(1:200 metric)

**BUILDING LAYOUT:
PASSING SOLUTION**

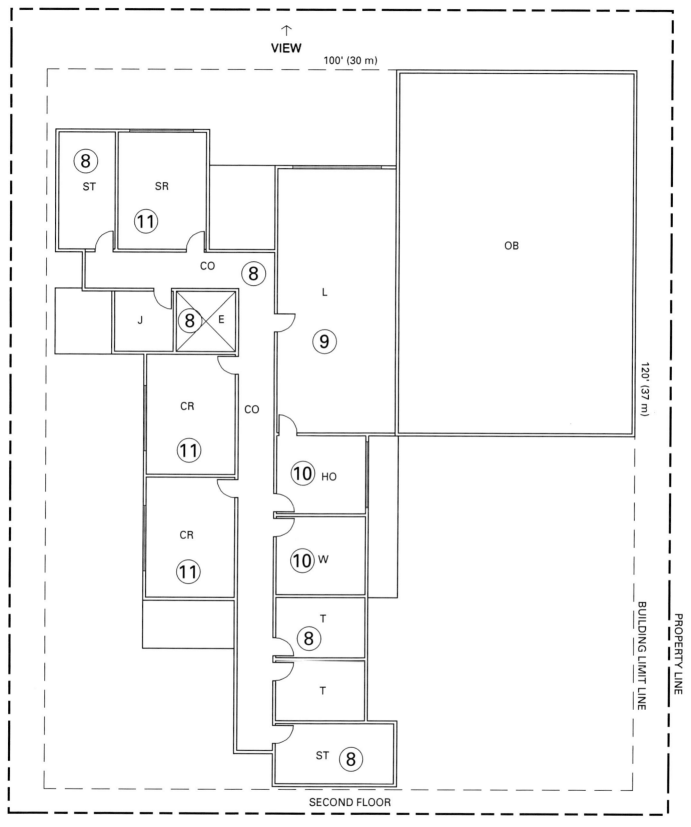

VIEW

100' (30 m)

8 ST

SR 11

CO 8

J 8 E

L 9

OB

CR 11 CO

CR 11

10 HO

10 W

T 8

T

ST 8

120' (37 m)

BUILDING LIMIT LINE

PROPERTY LINE

SECOND FLOOR

Scale: 1/16" = 1'-0"
(1:200 metric)

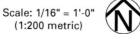

BUILDING LAYOUT:
PASSING SOLUTION

BUILDING PLAN: FAILING SOLUTION

Pitfalls

Note 1   The lounge is too far from the lobby.

Note 2   The storage room is not near the secretarial and administrator's offices, although this by itself would probably not cause the solution to fail.

Note 3   The janitor's closet is too small, possibly due to putting in a corridor as an afterthought to access the kitchen.

Note 4   There is no direct discharge to the outside from the stair near the lobby, violating a code requirement about stairs.

Note 5   The exit doors from the meeting/activity room open into the room instead of out into the lobby.

Note 6   There is no door from the administrator's office to the corridor, violating a code requirement about exits.

Note 7   The corridor to the kitchen is too narrow.

Note 8   On the second floor, the library workroom is not adjacent to the librarian's office, though the adjacency is required by the program. Also, the workroom is too small by about 50 ft² (4.6 m²), which is more than the 10% variance allowed.

Note 9   The library is slightly undersized and barely meets the 10% variance allowance at 817 ft² (75.9 m²). The main problem with the library is its poor aspect ratio; it is too long and narrow, although this by itself would probably not fail the solution.

Note 10 There is no exterior window provided in the north classroom.

Note 11 The dead-end corridor leading to the seminar room is longer than the allowable 20 ft (6100), exceeding the maximum by 6 in (150).

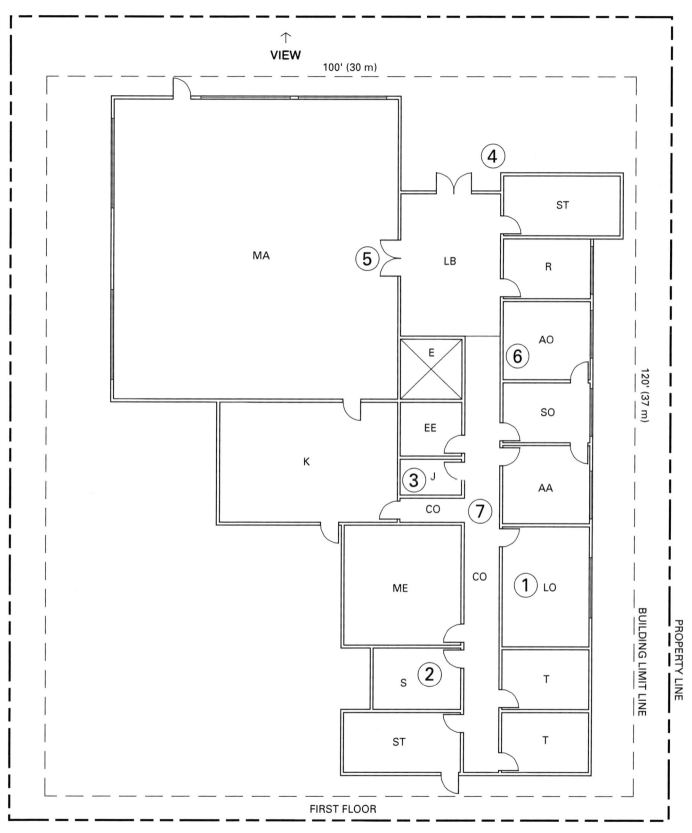

↑
VIEW

100' (30 m)

④

ST

R

⑤   LB

MA

AO

⑥

E

SO

EE

K   ③ J

AA

CO   ⑦

CO   ① LO

ME

T

② S

ST   T

120' (37 m)

BUILDING LIMIT LINE

PROPERTY LINE

FIRST FLOOR

Scale: 1/16" = 1'-0"   Ⓝ   **BUILDING LAYOUT:**
(1:200 metric)   **FAILING SOLUTION**

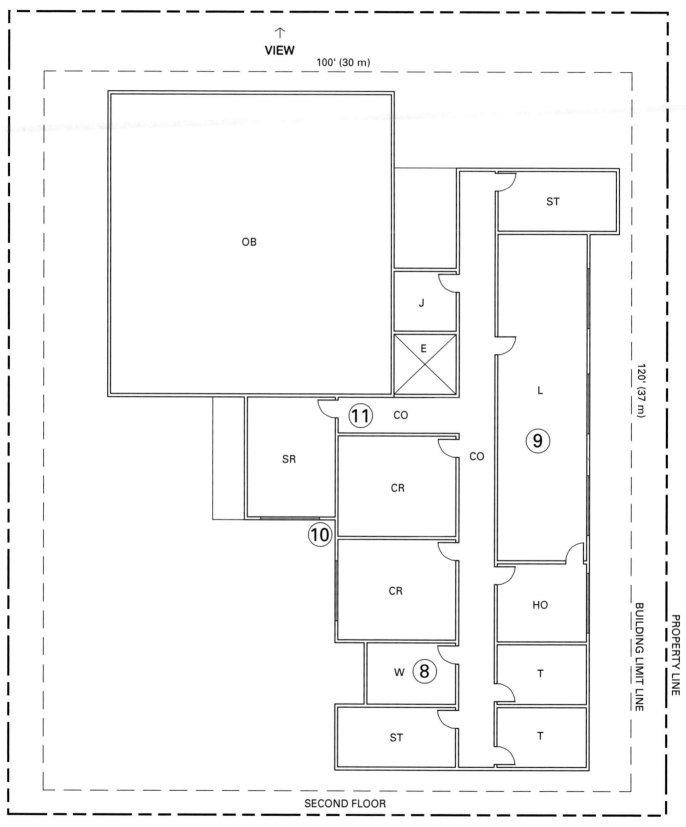

↑
VIEW
100' (30 m)

Scale: 1/16" = 1'-0"
(1:200 metric)

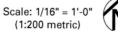

**BUILDING LAYOUT:
FAILING SOLUTION**

INTERIOR LAYOUT: PASSING SOLUTION

This vignette requires that the examinee establish wall locations to create the spaces required in the program and then place the required furniture in such a way that code requirements are satisfied.

Solving Approach

Step 1 Using the requirements of the program, it is best to start by roughly locating the walls that will define the various spaces. Most offices and rooms in the interior layout vignette require a minimum width from 12 ft to 14 ft (3.7 m to 4.3 m). There is the least flexibility about the location of the spaces that require windows, so these should be laid out first along the exterior wall.

Step 2 Estimate the most likely position of the other rooms that do not require windows, leaving the reception area with direct access to the entrance door. In this vignette, these two rooms could be located along either the south or the north perimeter walls, but the jog in the perimeter wall near the entry door 12 ft (3.7 m) from the north perimeter wall suggests these rooms would work well in the area between the jog and the north wall.

Step 3 Use the required direct access requirements to determine which interior room must be directly adjacent to the partner's office. Draw this room, estimating its required length. Its exact size can be adjusted later as required. This automatically locates the associate's office.

Step 4 Draw the remaining room, the workroom, up to the adjacent room. The size of this room can also be adjusted when the furniture is placed. Place the doors to the rooms.

Step 5 Place the required furniture in each room. Position it in a logical way. Make sure all the code clearances are satisfied. It is helpful to use sketch circles to verify that all clearances are correct. If necessary, modify the size and position of walls. Move the furniture into final position as required.

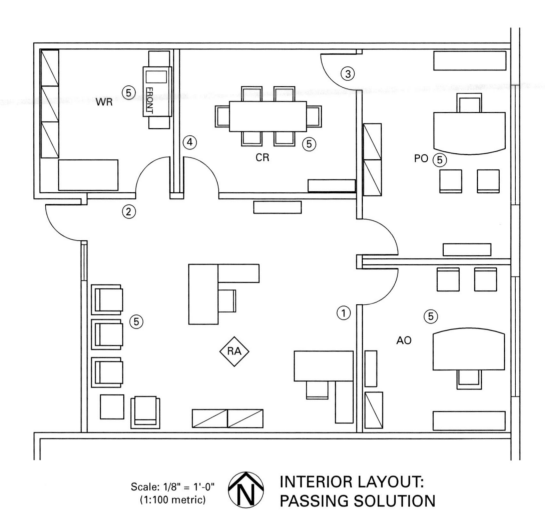

Scale: 1/8" = 1'-0"   **INTERIOR LAYOUT:**
(1:100 metric)   **PASSING SOLUTION**

INTERIOR LAYOUT: FAILING SOLUTION

Pitfalls

Note 1 This is an intermediate space, which is not allowed. All spaces must have direct access to the reception area.

Note 2 There is no direct access between the partner's office and the conference room.

Note 3 There is not enough accessibility clearance in the workroom at the strike side of the door; a minimum of 18 in (455) on the pull side is required.

Note 4 There is not enough accessibility clearance in the partner's office for the approach of the door; a minimum of 60 in (1525) is required.

Note 5 There is not enough accessibility clearance at the strike side of the door to the associate's office; a minimum of 12 in (305) on the push side is required.

Note 6 There is not enough turnaround space in the conference room; a minimum of 60 in (1525) is required.

Note 7 There is not enough space between the walls and the conference room chairs; a minimum of 36 in (914) is required.

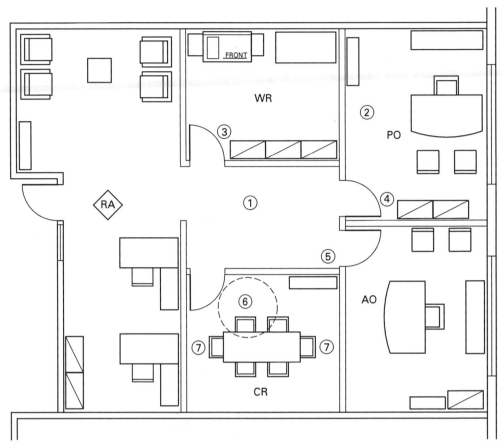

Scale: 1/8" = 1'-0"
(1:100 metric)

**INTERIOR LAYOUT:
FAILING SOLUTION**